"Scale is the holy grail of impact. Obidimma Ezezika demystifies it in this thoughtful book. Too often we assume that evidence alone leads to scale; but as Ezezika memorably puts it, innovations don't scale themselves. Using case studies, he frames scale through the lens of leadership and governance. This book on the methodology of scaling impact is timely given that global health policymakers need to do more with less."

— **Peter Singer**, *Professor Emeritus, University of Toronto; former CEO, Grand Challenges Canada; former Special Advisor to the Director-General, World Health Organization.*

"In over seventeen years of working across African health, environment, and development systems, I have seen firsthand how proven interventions stall not because the science is weak, but because the governance architecture to carry them is absent. Leadership in Global Health names this problem with precision and examines it with rigour. Drawing on cases that range from smallpox eradication to pandemic vaccine preparedness, Prof. Obidimma Ezezika demonstrates that scaling is not replication. It is the disciplined alignment of institutions, incentives, and accountability under conditions where no single actor holds control. This book will be essential reading for policymakers, implementation scientists, and practitioners who understand that the gap between evidence and impact is, at its core, a leadership gap."

— **Richard Munang**, *Head of the Global Programme on Crimes that Affect the Environment, United Nations Office on Drugs and Crime (UNODC), Adjunct Research Professor, Department of Epidemiology and Biostatistics, Western University*

"Dr. Ezezika convincingly argues that scale in global health is not a technical problem but a leadership one, requiring the alignment of institutions, incentives, and accountability across fragmented systems. Grounded in comparative case analysis and systems thinking, it offers scholars, policymakers, and practitioners a disciplined framework for understanding the decisions that determine whether health innovations transform systems at scale or remain pilot projects."

— **Kevin McKague**, *Canada Research Chair in Social Enterprise and Inclusive Markets and author of* Making Markets More Inclusive

Leadership in Global Health

Leadership in Global Health outlines the essential leadership principles that transform promising health interventions into global movements, offering a timely and compelling blueprint for leaders seeking to drive lasting, scalable change.

Grounded in decades of lessons from global health successes and failures, and illustrated through deeply analyzed, real-world case studies, the book reveals what happens when leadership meets coordinated action. These stories—from the eradication of smallpox and the large-scale delivery of malaria bed nets to the community-based innovations of Ethiopia's Health Extension Program and the lightning-fast COVID-19 vaccine rollout—show how leadership in global health is not one-size-fits-all, but rather dynamic, responsive, and deeply human. In an era where complex health challenges range from emerging pandemics to enduring inequities, the book centers the role of leadership—strategic, adaptive, and collaborative—as the critical engine for scaling health interventions, offering readers not only compelling narratives from the field, but also practical tools and reflections which give the book a forward-looking focus.

Offering a roadmap for developing the next generation of global health leaders equipped to thrive in multi-sectoral, rapidly evolving environments, it will be essential reading for students, scholars, and practitioners across Global Health, Public Health, Leadership and Development Studies.

Obidimma Ezezika is a global health scholar and faculty member at Western University in Canada, where he directs the Global Health & Innovation Lab. His work examines how leadership, institutions, and policy shape the ability of health innovations to scale and achieve population-level impact. He works with governments and global health institutions across Africa and beyond and has been recognized among Africa's leading scientific voices for contributions to global health research.

Leadership in Global Health

A Strategic Blueprint for Scalable Change

Obidimma Ezezika

Routledge
Taylor & Francis Group
LONDON AND NEW YORK

Designed cover image: Deposit Photos

First published 2027
by Routledge
4 Park Square, Milton Park, Abingdon, Oxon OX14 4RN

and by Routledge
605 Third Avenue, New York, NY 10158

Routledge is an imprint of the Taylor & Francis Group, an informa business

British Library Cataloguing-in-Publication Data
A catalogue record for this book is available from the British Library

ISBN: 978-1-041-16676-4 (hbk)
ISBN: 978-1-041-16590-3 (pbk)
ISBN: 978-1-003-68582-1 (ebk)

DOI: 10.4324/9781003685821

Typeset in Times New Roman
by codeMantra

**For my parents and my family,
and for those who lead under constraint.**

Contents

Figures

Tables

Acknowledgments

This book was strengthened through the thoughtful engagement of colleagues and collaborators whose insights shaped it at critical stages of its evolution.

Ombeva Malande provided constructive feedback on Part I, helping to refine the conceptual foundations of the manuscript. Edward Ameyaw offered detailed comments on Part III, sharpening its arguments and strengthening its coherence.

Research and editorial contributions were integral to this work. Lulya Woldetinsae provided research assistance for Chapter 9. Asa Wessner provided research assistance for Chapter 10. Michelle Ijomah provided research assistance for Chapter 11. Omolola Olorunbiyi offered feedback on Chapters 4 and 5, including comments on leadership framing, clarity, and reference consistency. Kishif Fatima assisted with reference editing and editorial review of select chapters. Thuwaraka Mohanakumar provided extensive support across multiple chapters, including proofreading, reference management, and figure preparation, helping to ensure precision and consistency throughout. Chisom Ezezika offered thoughtful reading and encouragement on the Introduction and Part I.

This work was developed within the intellectual community of the Global Health & Innovation Lab at Western University. I am grateful to the students and collaborators whose sustained inquiry sharpened the ideas that inform this book, and to Western University for providing the institutional environment in which this work could be undertaken.

I am especially grateful to Russell George at Routledge for his confidence in this project and for championing it through peer review and editorial approval. I also thank Amy Thomson for her guidance and professionalism throughout the submission process. I am also grateful to Emily Boyd for her careful copyediting and to Tiffany Cameron for her guidance and support during the production process.

I am sincerely grateful to all who contributed their time, care, and insight to this work.

Introduction

Scale as a Leadership Problem

In a modest clinic in rural Liberia, a community health worker prepares a cup of oral rehydration solution using Oral Rehydration Salts (ORS). The ingredients are simple: salt, sugar, and water. Yet the stakes are extraordinarily high. When used correctly, ORS dramatically reduces child mortality from diarrhoeal disease.[1] Despite this, more than 50 years after its introduction, ORS still reaches only a fraction of the children who need it globally, approximately one third.[2]

ORS is not a failure of science. It is a challenge of scale.

Global health is rich in proven solutions yet poor in sustained population-level impact. Interventions that demonstrate strong results in pilots routinely falter when confronted with the realities of health systems, political incentives, institutional capacity, and human behavior. The solution exists. The knowledge exists. What fails is the system that must carry it.

The central challenge is not the absence of evidence, but the persistent inability to scale effective interventions in ways that endure.

This book advances a simple proposition: scale is a leadership problem. Systems do not scale themselves. Institutions do not align automatically. Evidence does not embed on its own. Leadership is the mechanism through which systems are reconfigured to sustain change. Scaling is not a technical exercise alone. It is a leadership task that requires shaping systems, aligning incentives, stewarding relationships, and navigating complexity across time and levels of governance.

Purpose and Scope

The focus of this book is the leadership required to move health interventions from pilot to population. Across global health, progress at scale remains uneven, fragile, and frequently inequitable despite decades of investment in evidence generation and innovation. The gap between what works and what lasts reflects failures of governance, coordination, and institutional alignment more than failures of design.

Leadership, as used here, does not refer to formal authority or individual charisma. It refers to the capacity to set direction, mobilize actors, manage trade-offs, and sustain collective action within complex political and organizational environments. Whether scale is pursued through global coordination, national reform, regional partnership, or crisis response, leadership decisions shape whether interventions

DOI: 10.4324/9781003685821-1

become embedded in routine systems or remain temporary projects. Throughout this book, intervention refers to a defined program, policy instrument, guideline, or service delivery package designed to improve health outcomes.

Structure of the Book

The book is organized into four parts, each examining a distinct dimension of leadership at scale.

Part I: Foundations of Scale

This section establishes the conceptual architecture. It clarifies what scale is and what it is not, distinguishing piloting, expansion, and sustainability as analytically distinct phases with different leadership demands. Scale is framed not as replication or growth alone, but as a condition of constraint in which authority fragments, incentives diverge, and consequences reverberate across systems. The central argument is that technically sound interventions often stall not because evidence is weak, but because institutions, incentives, and governance arrangements are misaligned.

Part II: Leadership Under Constraint

This section examines five comparative cases that illuminate structural challenges of scale. Smallpox eradication demonstrates coordination without centralized enforcement. Malaria bed net delivery reveals the limits of durability when outcomes depend on behavior beyond formal command. MenAfriVac shows how leaders can redistribute complexity and risk to simplify frontline execution. Ethiopia's Health Extension Program illustrates the disciplined governance required for workforce scale. COVID-19 vaccine rollout exposes the difficulty of governing speed, equity, and legitimacy simultaneously. Across these cases, scale advances not through technical perfection but through leadership judgments about the allocation of authority, risk, and accountability.

Part III: Governing for Durable Scale

This section distills recurring leadership functions observed across successful efforts. It examines stakeholder alignment and coalition management, financing and resource mobilization, and adaptation through continuous learning and implementation science. The emphasis is diagnostic rather than prescriptive. These chapters illuminate the structural competencies required to stabilize distributed systems, manage trade-offs over time, and protect legitimacy as interventions mature.

Part IV: The Discipline of Leadership

This section shifts the unit of analysis from individual leaders to the institutional ecosystems that reproduce leadership capacity. It explores disciplined judgment under uncertainty, governance across distributed authority, and the political economy of leadership pipelines. As global health challenges grow more interconnected and politically contested, durable scale will depend not only on effective interventions, but on ecosystems capable of cultivating leaders who can govern complexity without illusion.

Audience

This book is written for policymakers, health system leaders, health managers, implementers, donors, and advisors responsible for translating evidence into sustained population-level impact. It is equally intended for implementation scientists, global and public health scholars, university lecturers, and postgraduate students seeking to understand how leadership, governance, and system design shape the durability of interventions. The framework also speaks to development partners, philanthropic actors, and cross-sector leaders working at the intersection of health, finance, and institutional reform.

By reframing scale as a leadership and systems challenge rather than a technical endpoint, the book provides a conceptual foundation for graduate training, professional education, and executive leadership development in global health and implementation science. It offers analytic tools and case-based insights for those designing, governing, studying, and teaching large-scale change across complex health systems.

The Persistence of the Know–Do Gap

Despite decades of evidence generation, the "know–do gap" remains one of the most persistent challenges in global health. Many rigorously validated interventions struggle to move beyond pilot settings.

Community-based models such as Care Groups have demonstrated substantial reductions in under-5 mortality in controlled settings.[3] Yet national replication often falters due to weak supervisory systems, limited financing, and poor integration across sectors.

Environmental health interventions reveal similar dynamics. Water, sanitation, and hygiene interventions reduce diarrhoeal disease when delivered with sufficient coverage and quality,[4] and baby-focused WASH strategies improve early child outcomes.[5] Global guidelines support hand hygiene as a foundational patient safety measure,[6,7] yet implementation remains inconsistent due to supply chain constraints, infrastructure gaps, and inconsistent institutional prioritization.[8]

Malaria control illustrates the same pattern. Insecticide-treated nets reduce child mortality,[9,10] but inconsistent use, procurement challenges, and emerging resistance continue to limit system-wide impact.

Maternal health follows similar trajectories. Skilled birth attendance reduces maternal mortality,[11] yet workforce shortages, geographic inequities, and fragile systems prevent consistent national uptake. As antiretroviral therapy expanded globally, including through major investments from the President's Emergency

Plan for AIDS Relief (PEPFAR) and the Global Fund, AIDS-related deaths fell markedly from their mid-2000s peak through 2018,[12] yet structural and political barriers persist for adolescents, rural populations, and key populations.

China's national Basic Public Health Services Program illustrates how aligning administrative incentives with primary health care priorities can support large-scale reform.[13–15] Performance-linked assessments aligned administrative incentives with primary health care priorities,[15] contributing to improvements in system performance. Such alignment, however, remains the exception rather than the norm.

Across regions and sectors, the pattern is consistent. Evidence alone does not produce scale. Sustained impact depends on leadership capable of aligning institutions, incentives, and accountability over time.

Leadership and the Architecture of Scale

Leadership shapes scale through governance, financing, coordination, and adaptive management. Major global health achievements illustrate how these functions operate in practice.

The MenAfriVac campaign across the African meningitis belt achieved near elimination of serogroup A meningitis through regional ownership, coordinated action, and sustained political commitment.[16–20] Gavi, the Vaccine Alliance, illustrates how predictable financing and structured governance arrangements have supported large-scale immunization efforts associated with millions of deaths averted over two decades.[21–23] PEPFAR's expansion of antiretroviral therapy combined strong global accountability with local delivery flexibility, enabling rapid treatment scale-up.[24,25]

National reforms further underscore the importance of leadership choices. Liberia's integration of salaried, supervised community health workers into primary health care expanded treatment coverage for childhood illnesses.[26] Integrated Population–Health–Environment models in East Africa required leadership capable of bridging sectoral mandates and coordinating across ministries.[27] China's primary health care reforms relied on performance incentives that aligned political and administrative objectives with health outcomes.[13–15]

In each case, scale emerged not because interventions were inherently scalable, but because leadership shaped systems to support sustained implementation.

The Leadership Imperative

The inverse is equally instructive. Early community health worker programs faltered when rapid expansion outpaced system capacity.[28,29] The Millennium Villages Project generated localized gains but failed to produce scalable system change due to its resource-intensive, externally driven model.[30] Maternal health voucher schemes deteriorated under weak oversight and accountability.[31] Knowledge translation initiatives failed to influence policy when implemented without leadership engagement.[32,33]

The lesson is consistent. Evidence without leadership does not scale.

The global health community has never had more tools, data, or technological capacity. Yet without leadership capable of aligning systems, navigating political realities, and sustaining long-term commitment, most interventions will remain confined to pilots.

Scale is rarely achieved by better pilots alone. It is achieved when leaders redesign systems to carry proven interventions into routine practice. The future of global health will depend less on the novelty of technical innovations than on the effectiveness of those who lead their disciplined integration into systems at scale.

The central question this book addresses is not whether scale is possible, but what kind of leadership makes it durable.

References

1. Bhutta ZA, Das JK, Walker N, Rizvi A, Campbell H, Rudan I, et al. Interventions to address deaths from childhood pneumonia and diarrhoea equitably: what works and at what cost? The Lancet. 2013 Apr 20;381(9875):1417–29. doi:10.1016/S0140–6736(13)60648-0
2. UNICEF. Diarrhoea [Internet]. 2023. Available from: https://data.unicef.org/topic/child-health/diarrhoeal-disease/
3. Perry H, Morrow M, Borger S, Weiss J, DeCoster M, Davis T, et al. Care groups I: an innovative community-based strategy for improving maternal, neonatal, and child health in resource-constrained settings. Glob Health Sci Pract. 2015 Sep 10;3(3):358–69. doi:10.9745/GHSP-D-15–00051
4. Wolf J, Hunter PR, Freeman MC, Cumming O, Clasen T, Bartram J, et al. Impact of drinking water, sanitation and handwashing with soap on childhood diarrhoeal disease: updated meta-analysis and meta-regression. Trop Med Int Health. 2018 May;23(5): 508–25. doi:10.1111/tmi.13051
5. Ngure FM, Reid BM, Humphrey JH, Mbuya MN, Pelto G, Stoltzfus RJ. Water, sanitation, and hygiene (WASH), environmental enteropathy, nutrition, and early child development: making the links. Ann N Y Acad Sci. 2014 Jan;1308:118–28. doi:10.1111/nyas.12330
6. Pittet D, Allegranzi B, Boyce J, World Health Organization World Alliance for Patient Safety First Global Patient Safety Challenge Core Group of Experts. The World Health Organization Guidelines on Hand Hygiene in Health Care and their consensus recommendations. Infect Control Hosp Epidemiol. 2009 Jul;30(7):611–22. doi:10.1086/600379
7. World Health Organization, editor. WHO guidelines on hand hygiene in health care: first global patient safety challenge: clean care is safer care. Geneva, Switzerland: World Health Organization, Patient Safety; 2009. 262 p.
8. Pittet D, Allegranzi B, Storr J, Bagheri Nejad S, Dziekan G, Leotsakos A, et al. Infection control as a major World Health Organization priority for developing countries. J Hosp Infect. 2008 Apr;68(4):285–92. doi:10.1016/j.jhin.2007.12.013
9. CDC. Malaria. Insecticide-treated nets [Internet]. 2024 [cited 2026 Jan 7]. Available from: https://www.cdc.gov/malaria/php/public-health-strategy/insecticide-treated-nets.html
10. Basiru A, Alozieuwa UB, Aboh MI, Usman UY, Nwaefulu ON, Okeke OP, et al. Utilization of insecticide-treated nets for malaria prevention among children in Africa: a systematic review and meta-analysis. Malar J. 2025 Oct 23;24(1):358. doi:10.1186/s12936-025-05599-w
11. Bhutta ZA, Das JK, Bahl R, Lawn JE, Salam RA, Paul VK, et al. Can available interventions end preventable deaths in mothers, newborn babies, and stillbirths, and at what cost? The Lancet. 2014 Jul 26;384(9940):347–70. doi:10.1016/S0140–6736(14)60792-3

12. UNAIDS. Communities at the Centre: Global AIDS Update [Internet]. Geneva: UNAIDS; 2019 Dec. p. 316. Report No. Available from: https://www.unaids.org/sites/default/files/media_asset/2019-global-AIDS-update_en.pdf
13. Cai C, Xiong S, Millett C, Xu J, Tian M, Hone T. Health and health system impacts of China's comprehensive primary healthcare reforms: a systematic review. Health Policy Plan. 2023 Jul 28;38(9):1064–78. doi:10.1093/heapol/czad058
14. Xiong S, Jiang W, Wang Y, Wang G, Zhang X, Hu C, et al. Co-designing interventions to strengthen the primary health care system for the management of hypertension and type 2 diabetes in China. Lancet Reg Health – West Pac. 2024 Aug 1;49. doi:10.1016/j.lanwpc.2024.101131
15. Yuan B, Balabanova D, Gao J, Tang S, Guo Y. Strengthening public health services to achieve universal health coverage in China. BMJ. 2019 Jun 21;365:l2358. doi:10.1136/bmj.l2358
16. Kristiansen PA, Diomandé F, Ba AK, Sanou I, Ouédraogo AS, Ouédraogo R, et al. Impact of the serogroup A meningococcal conjugate vaccine, MenAfriVac, on carriage and herd immunity. Clin Infect Dis Off Publ Infect Dis Soc Am. 2013 Feb;56(3):354–63. doi:10.1093/cid/cis892
17. Daugla DM, Gami JP, Gamougam K, Naibei N, Mbainadji L, Narbé M, et al. Effect of a serogroup A meningococcal conjugate vaccine (PsA–TT) on serogroup A meningococcal meningitis and carriage in Chad: a community study. The Lancet. 2014 Jan 4;383(9911):40–7. doi:10.1016/S0140–6736(13)61612-8
18. World Health Organization African Region. Meningitis A nearly eliminated in Africa through vaccination, reaching more than 235 million people [Internet]. 2016 [cited 2026 Jan 7]. Available from: https://www.afro.who.int/news/meningitis-nearly-eliminated-africa-through-vaccination-reaching-more-235-million-people
19. LaForce FM, Konde K, Viviani S, Préziosi MP. The Meningitis Vaccine Project. Vaccine. 2007 Sep 3;Meningococcal Meningitis in the African Meningitis Belt: Epidemiology and Vaccines25:A97–100. doi:10.1016/j.vaccine.2007.04.049
20. Ezezika O, Mengistu M, Lear T. Implementation of the Meningitis Vaccine Project in Africa: lessons for vaccine implementation programs. J Glob Health Rep. 2021 Nov 2; 5:e2021097. doi:10.29392/001c.29042
21. Gavi: The Vaccine Alliance. Annual Progress Report 2020 [Internet]. Geneva: Gavi The Vaccine Alliance; 2021. 52 p. Available from: https://www.gavi.org/sites/default/files/programmes-impact/our-impact/apr/Gavi-Progress-Report-2020.pdf
22. Sim SY, Watts E, Constenla D, Brenzel L, Patenaude BN. Return on investment from immunization against 10 pathogens in 94 low- and middle-income countries, 2011–30. Health Aff Proj Hope. 2020 Aug;39(8):1343–53. doi:10.1377/hlthaff.2020.00103
23. Gavi. Gavi's Investment Opportunity by numbers [Internet]. 2024 [cited 2026 Jan 7]. Available from: https://www.gavi.org/vaccineswork/gavi-investment-opportunity-by-numbers
24. El-Sadr WM, Holmes CB, Mugyenyi P, Thirumurthy H, Ellerbrock T, Ferris R, et al. Scale-up of HIV treatment through PEPFAR: a historic public health achievement. JAIDS J Acquir Immune Defic Syndr. 2012 Aug 15;60:S96. doi:10.1097/QAI.0b013e31825eb27b
25. Institute of Medicine. PEPFAR implementation: progress and promise. Washington, DC: The National Academies Press; 2007. 396 p.
26. White EE, Downey J, Sathananthan V, Kanjee Z, Kenny A, Waters A, et al. A community health worker intervention to increase childhood disease treatment coverage in rural Liberia: a controlled before-and-after evaluation. Am J Public Health. 2018 Sep;108(9):1252–9. doi:10.2105/AJPH.2018.304555

27. Ghiron L, Shillingi L, Kabiswa C, Ogonda G, Omimo A, Ntabona A, et al. Beginning with sustainable scale up in mind: initial results from a population, health and environment project in East Africa. Reprod Health Matters. 2014 Jan;22(43):84–92. doi:10.1016/S0968–8080(14)43761-3
28. Chang LW, Kagaayi J, Nakigozi G, Ssempijja V, Packer AH, Serwadda D, et al. Effect of peer health workers on AIDS care in Rakai, Uganda: a cluster-randomized trial. PLOS ONE. 2010 Jun 2;5(6):e10923. doi:10.1371/journal.pone.0010923
29. Ballard M, Montgomery P. Systematic review of interventions for improving the performance of community health workers in low-income and middle-income countries. BMJ Open. 2017 Oct 1;7(10):e014216. doi:10.1136/bmjopen-2016–014216 PubMed PMID: 29074507.
30. Mitchell S, Gelman A, Ross R, Chen J, Bari S, Huynh UK, et al. The Millennium Villages Project: a retrospective, observational, endline evaluation. Lancet Glob Health. 2018 May 1;6(5):e500–13. doi:10.1016/S2214-109X(18)30065-2
31. Bellows NM, Bellows BW, Warren C. Systematic review: the use of vouchers for reproductive health services in developing countries: systematic review. Trop Med Int Health. 2011;16(1):84–96. doi:10.1111/j.1365–3156.2010.02667.x
32. Moat KA, Lavis JN, Clancy SJ, El-Jardali F, Pantoja T, Knowledge Translation Platform Evaluation study team. Evidence briefs and deliberative dialogues: perceptions and intentions to act on what was learnt. Bull World Health Organ. 2014 Jan 1;92(1): 20–8. doi:10.2471/BLT.12.116806 PubMed PMID: 24391297
33. Paina L, Peters DH. Understanding pathways for scaling up health services through the lens of complex adaptive systems. Health Policy Plan. 2012 Aug;27(5):365–73. doi:10.1093/heapol/czr054

Part I

Foundations of Scale

Scaling health interventions is often described as expansion: Reaching more people, replicating what worked, and increasing coverage. Yet expansion alone does not produce durable impact. Interventions stall, fragment, or fade when they encounter institutional constraints, political trade-offs, and system complexity. Scale is not a moment of growth. It is a structural condition that tests whether systems can absorb and sustain change.

Part I establishes the conceptual foundation for understanding why scale so often falters. It clarifies that scaling is not a linear progression from pilot to replication, but a phased process shaped by different forms of uncertainty and constraint. Piloting tests feasibility. Expansion increases reach. Sustainability requires institutional alignment. Conflating these phases obscures the distinct leadership and system demands each introduces.

This section also advances a central proposition: scale succeeds only when evidence, leadership, and systems are aligned. Technical validity is necessary but insufficient. Leadership must sequence action, balance fidelity with adaptation, and govern trade-offs as complexity intensifies. At the same time, workforce capacity, financing arrangements, governance structures, supply chains, and information systems must function coherently. Expansion without alignment produces fragility.

Together, these chapters establish that durable scale is not achieved through replication alone. It emerges when interventions are embedded within institutional architectures capable of sustaining performance over time. The remainder of the book builds on this foundation by examining how leadership operates within these architectures under real conditions of constraint.

DOI: 10.4324/9781003685821-2

1 The Architecture of Scale

Scaling in global health requires more than expansion. It demands alignment between technical design, institutional capacity, and political leadership. Moving from pilot success to population-level impact involves managing increasing complexity while protecting the core mechanisms that make an intervention effective.

As argued elsewhere, no intervention scales itself; leaders scale interventions. Scale unfolds across three distinct phases: piloting, expansion, and sustainability. Each phase introduces new organizational, financial, and governance demands. Understanding these transitions is essential to moving from isolated success to durable impact.

This chapter examines the principles that predict scalable potential and the structural conditions that enable scale to endure.

Key Principles of Scaling in Global Health

Despite the diversity of health systems, several foundational principles consistently predict whether an intervention can scale.[1] These principles are not abstract slogans; they are patterns that emerge repeatedly across countries, disease areas, and delivery platforms. Table 1.1 summarizes these recurring principles and how they operate across contexts.

Adaptability

Adaptability is the capacity to modify an intervention to fit local needs while protecting its core components.[2,3] It is the discipline of knowing what must never change and what must change for the intervention to survive in a new context.

Consider a community organization in rural southwest Georgia tasked with implementing an evidence-based nutrition and physical activity program originally developed in a very different demographic and cultural setting.[3] The original protocol specified 90-minute group sessions delivered in a particular sequence, with standardized educational materials and homework activities. Very quickly, program leaders realized that many participants were juggling shift work, caregiving responsibilities, and limited transportation. Attendance began to drop.

DOI: 10.4324/9781003685821-3

Table 1.1 Real-World Examples by Principle

Principle	*Example*	*What Was Done*	*Impact*
Adaptability	Georgia's nutrition and physical education programs	Localization and accommodation for participants' needs	High satisfaction and attendance rate
Equity	Uganda and Tanzania maternal and newborn health using The Expanded Quality Management Using Information Power (EQUIP) strategy[13]	Coaching rural teams (or rural maternal health facilities)	+39% deliveries 26% and 8% increase in live births in Tanzania and Uganda, respectively[13]
Sustainability	Philippines Maternal, Neonatal, and Child Health (MNCH) scale plan	Local budget integration	+100% plan adoption among three local government units[7]
Systems Integration	National Health Service (NHS) "Your Care Needs You" model[8]	Embedded roles Aimed to ease transition from hospital to at-home care[8]	Higher adoption
Engagement	Philippines MNCH budgeting strategy	Co-design plans with policymakers and health care professionals	More funding
M&E (Monitoring & Evaluation)	Australia audits	Standardized feedback for researchers and policymakers	Course correction or identification of strategies for scaling up
Context Sensitivity	NHS "Your Care Needs You" model[8]	Cultural tailoring Multidisciplinary effort to tailor care to ward environment[14]	Feasibility

Faced with this reality, local implementers did not abandon the program; they adapted it. They shortened sessions to 45 minutes, moved some activities to evenings and weekends, rewrote examples using local foods and common daily routines, and paired sessions with low-cost exercise classes held in community centers and church halls. The *core mechanisms*—peer support, goal-setting, and structured education—remained intact. But the format, tone, and delivery were reshaped through continuous dialogue with participants.[3]

The result was not a loss of fidelity but a gain in fit. Engagement improved, satisfaction rates climbed to 80–100%, and several sites maintained over 50% participant attendance even at eight-week follow-up.[3] Adaptability, in this case, was not drift away from evidence; it was the deliberate translation of evidence into lived reality.

Similar dynamics appear in health systems guideline adaptation across low- and middle-income countries (LMICs). Breneol et al.[4] document how guideline developers used frameworks such as the Consolidated Framework for Implementation Research and the Knowledge-to-Action framework to iteratively adapt global recommendations to national and subnational realities—adding, for example, local examples, language translations, or task-sharing models to account for workforce constraints. When adaptation is systematic and purposeful, it becomes a core enabler of scale, not a threat to rigor.[2,4]

Yet adaptation alone does not guarantee fair distribution of benefits. Scale can expand reach while reproducing existing inequities.

Equity

The objective is not equality of identical inputs, but equity in the distribution of benefits. Equity focuses on ensuring fair access and outcomes across different populations, particularly those who are historically marginalized.[5,6] Many interventions "scale" in the narrow sense of geographic spread, yet leave behind the poorest, the most remote, or the least politically visible communities. Equity-centered scale demands that these groups be placed at the center rather than the periphery of scale-up efforts.

In Uganda, a maternal health quality improvement initiative provides a vivid illustration. Zamboni et al.[6] describe how program implementers recognized that early gains were concentrated in facilities serving relatively better-off populations. Rural facilities, often understaffed and under-resourced, lagged behind. Rather than treating this as an unfortunate side effect, the program redesigned its approach.

Intensified external support—through clinical and quality improvement coaching—was directed toward these rural facilities. Leadership engagement at district and facility levels was deliberately strengthened. Efforts were made to align quality improvement goals with national maternal health priorities so that rural facilities were not perceived as "outliers" but as central to national performance.[6]

This equity-driven scaling strategy produced measurable results. Facility deliveries increased by 39.3%, and the use of uterotonics immediately after birth increased by 35.3% in the targeted sites.[6] These are not abstract equity gains; they translate into lives saved in contexts where postpartum hemorrhage remains a leading cause of maternal death.

Equity, in this case, meant more than "reaching everyone eventually." It meant deliberately over-investing in the most disadvantaged settings to correct historical imbalances and shift the distribution of benefits.

Sustainability

Sustained impact requires that interventions be embedded into long-term funding, policy, and institutional structures.[5,7] Sustainability is not only about financial resources; it is about the degree to which an intervention becomes part of "how we do things here."

In the Philippines, the Investment Case approach to maternal, neonatal, and child health (MNCH) offers a powerful example.[7] The process began with a detailed analysis of local bottlenecks including shortages of midwives, gaps in essential newborn care, and weak referral systems. Local government units were then supported to design tailored packages of interventions and, crucially, to cost them.

The turning point came when these plans moved from paper into budgets. Municipal councils integrated 100% of the recommended strategies into their 2011 local investment plans for health, and these were subsequently reflected in annual operational plans.[7] Rather than depending on a time-limited project budget, MNCH investments were institutionalized within local government budget cycles.

This shift changed the conversation. Instead of asking, "Will the project continue when the donor leaves?", the question became, "How will we adjust our municipal plans next year to maintain and strengthen these services?" Sustainability was achieved not by securing a perpetual external grant but by reshaping local planning and budgeting routines.

Systems Integration

Systems integration ensures that interventions align with existing health system structures and workflows rather than creating parallel systems that compete for time, data, and resources.[6,8]

In the UK, a complex patient-centered care model targeting people with multiple long-term conditions sought to improve coordination and person-centeredness across fragmented services.[8] The design team could have created a stand-alone program with its own staff, data, and reporting structures. Instead, they made a strategic choice: to embed the intervention within the National Health Service's existing governance systems.

Care coordination roles were adapted from existing job descriptions rather than invented from scratch. Routine data systems were used for monitoring outcomes, avoiding the burden of duplicate data entry. Governance and accountability flowed through existing committees and reporting lines.[8]

This integration did not eliminate all challenges, but it facilitated smoother adoption. Staff could see how the intervention fit into their day-to-day work and existing performance structures. Rather than becoming an "extra project," it became a way of delivering better care within the system they already inhabited.

Stakeholder Engagement

Stakeholder engagement is more than a box-ticking exercise. Real engagement means that communities, policymakers, practitioners, and other actors influence decisions, not merely receive information.[2,7]

The Philippines Investment Case process again illustrates this principle. Local policymakers were not simply invited to approve a pre-designed package; they co-identified service delivery gaps and co-developed intervention strategies.[7] Midwives, nurses, and facility managers contributed insights on where women were lost along the continuum of care. Community representatives could speak to financial and geographic barriers that shaped care-seeking behavior.

Because local actors participated in defining the problem and the solution, their ownership of the resulting plans was strong. When it came time to integrate strategies into municipal budgets, these were not "external recommendations" but "our plans." This sense of authorship was key to the full integration of Investment Case recommendations and the subsequent increases in budget allocations for essential newborn care and midwife staffing.[7]

In Kenya's Integrated Early Childhood Development (ECD) program in informal settlements, Ssewanyana et al.[9] similarly show how ongoing dialogue with caregivers, community health volunteers, teachers, and local officials surfaced both enablers (such as community commitment to child development) and barriers (such as poverty and staff turnover). This engagement did not merely inform implementation; it shaped it.

Monitoring and Evaluation

Monitoring and evaluation (M&E) embed continuous learning into the scaling process.[5,6] When implemented well, M&E allows implementers and policymakers to detect implementation breakdowns early and adjust accordingly.

Australian scale-up initiatives reviewed by Milat et al.[5] often used standardized reporting templates, regular performance review meetings, and feedback loops to track progress. For instance, health promotion programs might monitor reach, fidelity, and short-term behavior change indicators on a quarterly basis. Where uptake was low, teams could investigate whether the problem lay in community engagement, staff capacity, or logistical barriers.

The key insight is that M&E is not only for accountability upward—to funders or national authorities—but also for learning outward and downward, to implementers and communities. When feedback is shared transparently, it can strengthen trust and shared responsibility.

Context Sensitivity

Context sensitivity recognizes that interventions are implemented into living systems—marked by political dynamics, cultural norms, organizational histories, and local priorities.[3,8] Treating context as "noise" to be controlled rather than as a central feature of implementation underestimates its power.

Mills et al.[8] highlight how a logic model for a complex care intervention evolved as implementers encountered different organizational cultures across sites. In some settings, hierarchical structures required explicit authorization from senior leadership before staff felt free to experiment with new practices. In others, more distributed leadership models allowed frontline teams to adapt swiftly. Context sensitivity meant recognizing these differences and tailoring facilitation, communication, and support strategies accordingly.

Similarly, Carvalho et al.[3] show how community-based programs in the US South had to account for local histories of mistrust of external institutions, transportation challenges in rural areas, and differing norms around diet and physical activity. Interventions that acknowledged and worked with these contextual realities, rather than ignoring them, were more likely to be accepted and sustained.

Together, these principles highlight that scaling is not simply technical expansion—it is a dynamic, relational, and context-dependent process requiring leadership, flexibility, and systems thinking.

Piloting, Expansion, and Sustainability: Understanding the Differences

Although often conflated, piloting, expansion, and sustainability are distinct phases of scaling, each with different goals, activities, and challenges. Misunderstanding these phases is one of the most common reasons interventions fail to scale. Many global health projects treat scale-up as a binary: first "pilot," then "go to scale." The reality is more granular—and more demanding. Figure 1.1 illustrates how these phases differ and build upon one another, drawing on broader guidance on scalability and scaling-up strategy.[1,5,15]

The pilot phase tests feasibility and contextual fit; expansion increases reach and coordination complexity; sustainability embeds the intervention into routine governance, financing, and service delivery systems.

The Pilot Phase: Testing the Promise of an Idea

The pilot phase tests feasibility, usability, and initial acceptability in a small number of sites. It answers questions such as: Can frontline workers realistically deliver this intervention? Do users understand and value it? What unforeseen barriers and unintended consequences arise?

In Ethiopia, the pilot implementation of the Primary Health Care Clinical Guidelines (EPHCG) across 18 health centers offers a concrete illustration.[10] The guidelines aimed to support integrated management of non-communicable diseases (NCDs) and mental health conditions at the primary care level. During the pilot, teams developed training packages, delivered them to health workers, and collected feedback on how usable and relevant the guidelines were in busy, resource-constrained settings.

Health workers reported that the guidelines were helpful but time-consuming to use in the context of large patient loads.[10] Some struggled to integrate mental

Figure 1.1 The Three Phases of Scaling: Pilot, Expansion, and Sustainability

health assessments into routine visits. Others raised concerns about the availability of medications recommended in the guidelines. These insights were critical: they made visible the gap between the idealized intervention model and the realities of frontline service delivery.

A very different type of pilot was the launch of the Kisiizi Community-Based Health Insurance (CBHI) scheme in rural Uganda.[11] Here, the goal was to test whether community groups—Bataka groups with deep traditions of mutual support—would accept and sustain prepayment for health services. The pilot focused on mobilizing local groups, forming scheme management structures, and enrolling members. Feasibility hinged not on training health workers but on aligning the insurance concept with existing social norms. Early success came from the fact that the scheme did not introduce a foreign logic of individual insurance, but rather built on long-standing practices of collective risk-sharing.[11]

In both cases, the pilot phase was not just about demonstrating "success." It was about surfacing what needed to change—whether in guidelines, training, communication, or institutional arrangements—before any attempt at wider expansion.

The Expansion Phase: Moving from Islands of Success to Larger Coverage

The expansion phase moves interventions beyond the pilot area through broader training, multi-sector coordination, and policy alignment.[4,9,10] It is the phase where complexity increases sharply: more sites, more actors, more variability.

In Ethiopia, scaling up the Primary Health Care Guidelines required cascaded training-of-trainers models, integration with regional health bureau plans, and coordination with district leadership.[10] While training coverage increased substantially, fidelity of implementation varied widely. In districts where leadership was engaged and supportive, guidelines were more consistently used in routine care. In others, competing priorities and resource shortages limited uptake.

Guideline implementation efforts documented by Breneol et al.[4] show similar dynamics across multiple LMICs. Expansion often entails combining several implementation strategies—education, audit and feedback, local champions, and ongoing mentorship. The Expert Recommendations for Implementing Change (ERIC) project provides a menu of such strategies, but their impact depends heavily on local capacity and resources.

In Kenya, the expansion of an Integrated Early Childhood Development (ECD) program into an informal settlement required coordination across health, education, and social protection sectors.[9] Early iterations revealed mismatches between national ECD policies and the lived realities of families in informal settlements, who faced unstable housing, insecure income, and limited access to services. Expansion was successful where program implementers partnered closely with community organizations, adapted delivery platforms (e.g., using community centers and faith-based venues), and worked within existing decentralized governance systems.[9]

Expansion, then, is not merely "doing more of the same." It is a re-engineering phase, in which interventions are modified, institutional arrangements are negotiated, and implementation strategies are layered to cope with variation across sites.

The Sustainability Phase: Embedding the Intervention into the Fabric of the System

The sustainability phase embeds the intervention into routine health system operations[12], long-term financing[11], and governance structures.[9] The question here shifts from "How do we expand?" to "How do we endure?"

For the Kisiizi CBHI scheme, sustainability involved several intertwined elements: maintaining community trust, ensuring that premiums remained affordable, managing defaults, and dealing with the practical challenges of distance to the hospital.[11] Over time, the scheme became integrated into regional financing strategies and maintained stable enrollment, helping to reduce the burden of unpaid care on the hospital and providing a safety net for participating households.

In Kenya's ECD program, sustainability meant institutionalizing practices within existing community structures and service platforms, rather than relying solely on a stand-alone project team.[9] This involved embedding ECD activities into the routines of community health workers, early childhood centers, and local planning and budgeting systems. Stakeholders emphasized that sustaining ECD required attention to staff retention, ongoing training, and long-term funding—not just initial enthusiasm.

Continuing professional education (CPE) programs in LMICs reveal another angle on sustainability. Hill et al.[12] found that CPE efforts were more likely to be sustained when they were led or co-led by LMIC institutions, embedded within existing governance and funding arrangements, and supported by long-term partnerships rather than short-term training missions. Sustainability here is as much about power and ownership as it is about technical design.

Understanding these phases clarifies that scaling is not a single leap but a progression: testing what works, expanding reach, and embedding practices into the health system for the long haul.

Barriers and Enablers of Scale

Across the three phases, several recurring barriers emerge in global health scale-up. Weak infrastructure and supply chains can compromise even the most elegant interventions. Insufficient staffing and high workloads undermine training efforts and reduce adherence to new guidelines.[10] Political resistance may stall policy alignment, especially when interventions challenge existing interests or require reallocation of resources. Fragmented systems and poor coordination erode the coherence needed for multi-sectoral interventions such as ECD.[9] Funding cuts or shifts in donor priorities can destabilize programs just as they reach maturity. These breakdown points recur across settings and phases, as illustrated in Figure 1.2, which maps common system-level risks across pilot, expansion, and sustainability phases and highlights the corresponding leadership actions required to maintain alignment and achieve durable scale.

The literature is clear: technical solutions alone cannot overcome systemic constraints.

Yet the enablers of successful scale are equally consistent. Visionary leadership at national, district, facility, and community levels creates the political and

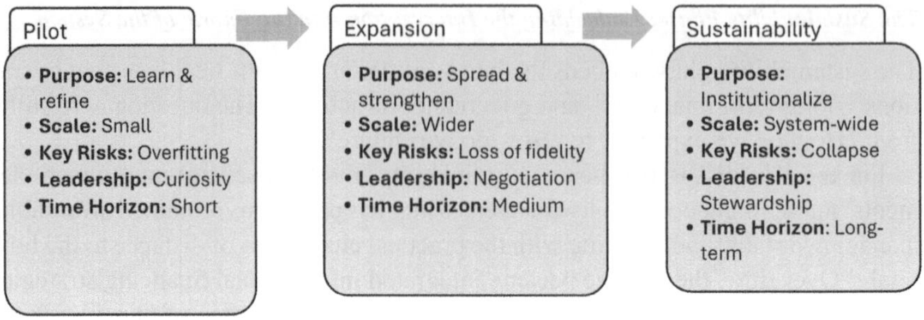

Figure 1.2 Core Risks and Leadership Tasks Across the Scaling Journey

organizational space for change. Policy alignment reduces friction and sends a clear signal that an intervention is not a passing fad but a strategic priority.[7,10] Adaptive design, grounded in principles of flexibility and context sensitivity, enables interventions to remain relevant across diverse settings.[3,8]

Community ownership and social cohesion, as seen in the Kisiizi CBHI scheme, provide a social foundation for sustained engagement.[11] Strong institutional support and strategic partnerships—such as those underlying LMIC-led CPE collaborations—enable capacity-building and continuity.[12] Robust monitoring and feedback systems facilitate course correction and reinforce accountability.[5,6]

Ethiopia's guideline expansion benefited from strong Ministry of Health commitment, Ethiopia's ECD work flourished through cross-sector collaboration and alignment with local structures, and Uganda's community-based insurance scheme sustained itself through trusted leadership and group solidarity.[9–11] These examples underscore a central insight: scaling succeeds when technical design and political, social, and institutional capabilities reinforce each other. Scaling fails when these dimensions fall out of alignment.

Leadership Moves

Leadership for scale begins by treating scale not as simple expansion, but as the deliberate alignment of intervention design, institutional capacity, political commitment, and long-term system ownership.

- **Define scale before expanding.** Leaders should clarify whether they are piloting, expanding, or sustaining an intervention. Each phase has different demands. Pilots test feasibility and fit; expansion increases reach and complexity; sustainability embeds the intervention into routine systems, budgets, and governance.
- **Protect the core while adapting the form.** Not every feature of a pilot needs to travel. Leaders must identify the core mechanisms that produce impact and distinguish them from delivery forms that can be modified across settings, populations, and institutions.

- **Design for equity from the beginning.** Scale should not be judged only by reach. Leaders must ask who benefits, who is left behind, and whether expansion is correcting or reproducing existing inequities. Equity may require deliberate over-investment in disadvantaged settings.
- **Build ownership into the system.** Durable scale depends on whether local institutions, communities, and frontline actors see the intervention as their own. Engagement should shape decisions, not merely communicate decisions already made.
- **Integrate rather than bypass.** Leaders should avoid creating parallel systems that compete with existing workflows, data routines, financing channels, and accountability structures. Scale is more likely to endure when interventions become part of how the system already works.
- **Use monitoring as a leadership tool.** Monitoring and evaluation should not be treated only as reporting requirements. Feedback systems help leaders detect breakdowns, adapt implementation, strengthen accountability, and maintain legitimacy over time.
- **Align what the intervention requires with what the system can carry.** Scaling fails when technical design, workforce capacity, infrastructure, financing, political support, and community trust fall out of alignment. The leadership task is to make these conditions reinforce one another before fragility becomes failure.

References

1. Richard K, Johannes FL. Paper prepared for the Scaling Community of Practice [Internet]. 2021 Dec p. 30. Available from: https://www.scalingcommunityofpractice.com/wp-content/uploads/bp-attachments/8991/Scaling-Principles-Paper-final-13-Dec-21.pdf
2. Aarons GA, Sklar M, Mustanski B, Benbow N, Brown CH. "Scaling-out" evidence-based interventions to new populations or new health care delivery systems. Implementation Sci. 2017 Sep 6;12(1):111.
3. Carvalho ML, Honeycutt S, Escoffery C, Glanz K, Sabbs D, Kegler MC. Balancing fidelity and adaptation: implementing evidence-based chronic disease prevention programs. Journal of Public Health Management and Practice. 2013 Aug;19(4):348.
4. Breneol S, Curran JA, Marten R, Minocha K, Johnson C, Wong H, et al. Strategies to adapt and implement health system guidelines and recommendations: a scoping review. Health Res Policy Sys. 2022 Jun 15;20(1):64.
5. Milat AJ, King L, Bauman AE, Redman S. The concept of scalability: increasing the scale and potential adoption of health promotion interventions into policy and practice. Health Promot Int. 2013 Sep 1;28(3):285–98.
6. Zamboni K, Baker U, Tyagi M, Schellenberg J, Hill Z, Hanson C. How and under what circumstances do quality improvement collaboratives lead to better outcomes? A systematic review. Implementation Sci. 2020 May 4;15(1):27.
7. La Vincente S, Aldaba B, Firth S, Kraft A, Jimenez-Soto E, Clark A. Supporting local planning and budgeting for maternal, neonatal and child health in the Philippines. Health Res Policy Sys. 2013 Jan 23;11(1):3.
8. Mills T, Shannon R, O'Hara J, Lawton R, Sheard L. Development of a "real-world" logic model through testing the feasibility of a complex healthcare intervention: the challenge of reconciling scalability and context-sensitivity. Evaluation. 2022 Jan 1;28(1):113–31.

9. Ssewanyana D, Martin MC, Angwenyi V, Kabue M, Proulx K, Zhang L, et al. Stakeholders' perspectives of enablers and barriers to successfully implementing an integrated early childhood development program in an informal urban settlement in Kenya. SAGE Open [Internet]. 2023 Nov 16 [cited 2026 Jan 9]; Available from: https://journals.sagepub.com/doi/10.1177/21582440231208986
10. Bekele A, Alem A, Seward N, Eshetu T, Gebremariam TH, Getachew Y, et al. Barriers and enablers to improving integrated primary healthcare for non-communicable diseases and mental health conditions in Ethiopia: a mixed methods study. BMC Prim Care. 2024 Jun 11;25(1):211.
11. Kakama AA, Namyalo PK, Basaza RK. Feasibility and desirability of scaling up Community-based Health Insurance (CBHI) in rural communities in Uganda: lessons from Kisiizi Hospital CBHI scheme. BMC Health Serv Res. 2020 Jul 17;20(1):662.
12. Hill E, Gurbutt D, Makuloluwa T, Gordon M, Georgiou R, Roddam H, et al. Collaborative healthcare education programmes for continuing professional education in low and middle-income countries: a Best Evidence Medical Education (BEME) systematic review. BEME Guide No. 65. Medical Teacher. 2021 Nov 2;43(11):1228–41.
13. Waiswa P, Manzi F, Mbaruku G, Rowe AK, Marx M, Tomson G, et al. Effects of the EQUIP quasi-experimental study testing a collaborative quality improvement approach for maternal and newborn health care in Tanzania and Uganda. Implement Sci. 2017 Jul 18;12(1):89.
14. Baxter R, Murray J, O'Hara JK, Hewitt C, Richardson G, Cockayne S, et al. Improving patient experience and safety at transitions of care through the Your Care Needs You (YCNY) intervention: a study protocol for a cluster randomised controlled feasibility trial. Pilot Feasibility Stud. 2020 Sep 2;6(1):123.
15. Sexual and Reproductive Health and Research (SRH). Nine steps for developing a scaling-up strategy [Internet]. Geneva: World Health Organization; 2010 Sep p. 42. Available from: https://iris.who.int/server/api/core/bitstreams/82b17330-72b9-42b3-8a05-dd5f6cb5e29b/content

2 Leadership as System-Level Enabler

Leadership as the System-Level Enabler of Scale

Scaling health interventions rarely fails for technical reasons alone. Financing, infrastructure, and workforce capacity matter, but they do not explain why similar interventions achieve durable impact in some contexts and fragment in others. Leadership is what distinguishes sustained scale.

Leadership shapes how technical resources are mobilized, institutions align around shared priorities, and complexity is governed as interventions expand beyond pilot settings. It influences which interventions are prioritized for expansion, how they are framed politically and socially, and whether they are adapted, sustained, or abandoned as challenges emerge. Leadership also shapes the implementation climate by signaling commitment, allocating authority, and fostering accountability—factors widely recognized as central to implementation effectiveness.[1]

In scale-up contexts, leadership is not individual charisma or positional authority alone. It is a system-level function that operates through governance arrangements, institutional cultures, and relationships across levels of the health system. As interventions expand, heterogeneity increases, resource constraints intensify, and decisions that were once technical become political. Informal processes must be formalized, and learning that once occurred organically must be institutionalized. Leadership is the mechanism through which coherence is maintained amid this growing complexity. When leadership is weak or misaligned, scale-up efforts risk fragmentation, loss of fidelity, and erosion of legitimacy.

This chapter examines leadership as a core mechanism of scale-up, drawing on comparative global health cases summarized in Table 2.1.

The analysis is organized around three interrelated leadership functions that consistently emerge across successful scale-up efforts: vision-setting and strategic direction; the deliberate sequencing of adaptive and directive leadership; and the integration of evidence-based interventions with disciplined innovation in delivery, governance, and learning. Together, these functions illuminate how leadership enables the transition from promising interventions to durable, system-level change. Figure 2.1 presents a systems view of leadership as the engine that aligns vision, governance, evidence, and learning to enable sustained scale.

DOI: 10.4324/9781003685821-4

Table 2.1 Leadership Functions Across Phases of Health Intervention Scale-Up

Scale-Up Phase	*Primary Leadership Function*	*Dominant Leadership Style*	*Key Risks if Leadership Is Weak*	*Illustrative Case Examples*
Initiation and Early Expansion	Vision-setting and strategic framing	Directive	Fragmentation and lack of buy-in	Ethiopia HSEP; WHO GPW13
Rapid Expansion and Alignment	Governance and coordination	Directive with accountability	Duplication and inconsistent delivery	Côte d'Ivoire COVID-19 response; CDC Tips
Contextualization and Learning	Adaptation and problem-solving	Adaptive	Resistance and loss of relevance	Smallpox eradication; Surgical Safety Checklist
Institutionalization	Embedding into systems and routines	Hybrid	Dependence on individuals	Rwanda CBHI; ORS integration
Sustainability and Resilience	Evidence stewardship and system learning	Adaptive with oversight	Declining quality and inequity	GBD platform; WHO GPW13 monitoring

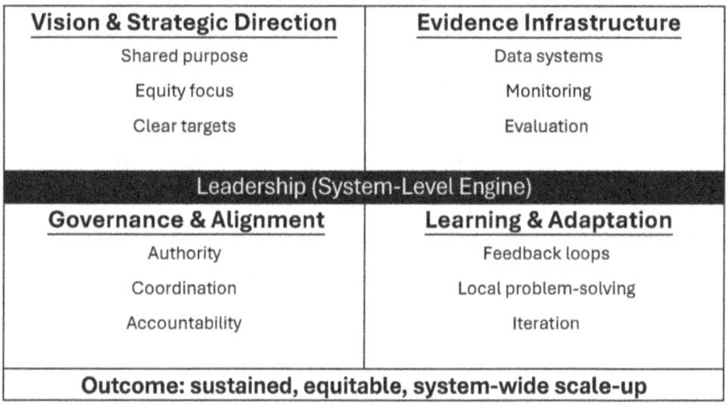

Figure 2.1 Leadership as the Engine of Health Intervention Scale-Up

Figure 2.1 illustrates how leadership aligns vision, governance, evidence infrastructure, and learning to enable sustained and equitable scale.

Vision-Setting and Strategic Direction

Vision as a Coordinating Force in Scale-Up

In scale-up contexts, vision plays a fundamentally different role, serving functions that extend well beyond those required in small-scale implementation. At scale, vision functions as a coordinating force that aligns diverse actors who may not share institutional mandates, professional cultures, or incentives. Ministries of health, finance departments, donors, non-governmental organizations (NGOs), frontline providers, and communities all participate in scale-up processes, often with competing priorities. A clearly articulated vision provides a shared reference point that reduces ambiguity and enables collective decision-making across these actors.

For example, the Ethiopian Health Extension Program provides a clear illustration of vision operating as a system-level coordination mechanism. Under the leadership of Kesete-Birhan Admasu, Ethiopia articulated a national vision of universal primary health care grounded in community-based delivery, prevention, and equity.[2] This vision was embedded within the Health Sector Development Programme and translated into explicit commitments to deploy health extension workers to rural areas, construct health posts, and integrate community engagement into service delivery. Vision in this context aligned political leadership, technical experts, and local administrators around a long-term transformation agenda that extended beyond individual projects or funding cycles.

A similar dynamic is evident in Rwanda's national scale-up of community-based health insurance.[3] Leadership framed health insurance as a mechanism for social solidarity and financial protection rather than as a market-based product. This framing helped build trust among communities and legitimized redistributive policies, including premium subsidies for poorer households. By anchoring scale-up in a shared moral and social purpose, leadership reduced resistance and fostered sustained participation across socioeconomic groups.[4]

Translating Vision into Strategic Direction

Vision alone is insufficient to produce scale. Leaders must translate vision into strategic direction by defining priorities, setting measurable goals, establishing governance arrangements, and creating accountability mechanisms. Strategic direction operationalizes vision by clarifying what will be done, by whom, and by when. Without this translation, vision risks remaining aspirational rather than actionable.

The World Health Organization (WHO)'s Thirteenth General Programme of Work (GPW13) illustrates how strategic direction can translate a long-standing normative commitment to health equity into operational change.[5] Under the leadership of Dr. Tedros Adhanom Ghebreyesus, the WHO reframed the aspiration of "health for all" through the triple billion targets, establishing concrete benchmarks for universal health coverage, emergency preparedness, and population well-being. Achieving these targets required internal institutional reform, including changes to planning, budgeting, recruitment, and performance management systems, as well as expanded use of data and delivery dashboards. Strategic direction in this case enabled a large and complex organization to align its activities around shared objectives while allowing country offices and regional entities flexibility in how those objectives were pursued in diverse contexts.

Strategic direction was also critical in national crisis responses. Côte d'Ivoire's COVID-19 Strategic Preparedness and Response Project established explicit targets for vaccination coverage and health system strengthening.[6] When initial assumptions about imported cases proved inaccurate and community transmission increased, leadership revised operational strategies while maintaining overarching goals. This capacity to adapt tactics without losing strategic coherence contributed to rapid expansion of vaccination sites and daily dose administration.

Vision, Equity, and Moral Authority

Vision becomes particularly powerful in scale-up when it is grounded in equity and moral authority. Scale-up efforts often involve difficult trade-offs, including decisions about resource allocation, prioritization of populations, and tolerance for short-term inefficiencies. Equity-oriented vision provides leaders with the legitimacy to sustain commitment in the face of these challenges.

Paul Farmer's leadership through Partners In Health exemplifies the role of moral vision in enabling scale. By framing health care as a human right, Farmer challenged prevailing assumptions about feasibility in resource-constrained settings.[7] This vision justified investments in community health workers, social support, and long-term accompaniment. Evidence generated through these programs later influenced global guidelines for tuberculosis and multidrug-resistant tuberculosis care, demonstrating how moral vision can reshape both practice and policy at scale.[8,9]

The global smallpox eradication program similarly relied on a vision of shared responsibility and global solidarity. Leaders framed eradication as a collective moral obligation, sustaining political commitment across countries with diverse interests and capacities.[10] In both cases, vision functioned not only as a guide for action but also as a source of moral authority that enabled leaders to mobilize resources and sustain effort over extended periods. While vision establishes the moral authority and shared direction necessary for collective commitment, achieving system-wide scale depends on how leadership is exercised at the system level, particularly in the balance between directive action and adaptive engagement over time.

Adaptive and Directive Leadership in Scale-Up

Scale-Up as an Adaptive Leadership Challenge

Scaling up health interventions presents adaptive challenges that cannot be resolved through technical expertise alone. Adaptive challenges involve changes in behaviors, norms, and relationships within systems and therefore require learning, negotiation, and shifts in values rather than straightforward application of known solutions.[11] Leadership in scale-up contexts involves mobilizing stakeholders to confront uncertainty and engage in collective problem-solving.

Many scale-up efforts falter when leaders treat adaptive challenges as technical problems. Resistance from health workers may be addressed through additional training when underlying issues relate to trust or professional identity. Community hesitancy may be addressed through information campaigns when deeper concerns about legitimacy or historical exclusion remain unaddressed. Effective leaders recognize these dynamics and adjust their leadership approach accordingly. Recognizing adaptive dynamics does not eliminate the need for authority; rather, system-level leadership requires clarity about when directive action is necessary to create alignment, mobilize resources, and enable collective response at scale.

The Role of Directive Leadership

Directive leadership remains essential in scale-up, particularly when coordination, speed, and standardization are required. Directive leadership clarifies authority, establishes rules, and mobilizes resources. It is especially valuable during crises or when system-wide alignment is necessary.

Ethiopia's Health Extension Program benefited from strong directive leadership during its early expansion. High-level political commitment ensured that ministries aligned around shared goals and that resources were mobilized at scale.[2] Similarly, Côte d'Ivoire's COVID-19 response relied on centralized coordination through a national steering committee, enabling rapid expansion of vaccination capacity and coordinated engagement with international partners.[6,12]

Furthermore, The Centers for Disease Control and Prevention's Tips From Former Smokers campaign provides another example of directive leadership enabling scale. Clear mandates, standardized messaging, and explicit calls to action ensured consistency across jurisdictions.[13] This directive approach contributed to substantial population-level outcomes, including an estimated 16.4 million quit attempts and over 1 million sustained quits.[14,15]

Adaptive Leadership and Learning at Scale

Adaptive leadership becomes critical when scale-up encounters heterogeneity and uncertainty. As interventions expand, they must be tailored to diverse institutional and cultural contexts. Adaptive leadership emphasizes listening, experimentation, and learning from feedback rather than rigid adherence to predefined plans.

The smallpox eradication program demonstrates adaptive leadership in practice. Field observations revealed that mass vaccination alone was insufficient in settings with limited vaccine supply and weak infrastructure. Leaders adapted strategy toward surveillance and containment, using real-time data and iterative learning to refine approaches.[10,16] This adaptive shift was instrumental in achieving global eradication.

The implementation of the WHO Surgical Safety Checklist further illustrates adaptive leadership. While the checklist provided standardized protocols, its effectiveness depended on local adaptation and cultural change. Leaders worked through local champions, addressed professional resistance, and used feedback mechanisms and audits to improve adherence.[17,18] Adaptive leadership enabled the checklist to be embedded within diverse surgical environments while preserving its core safety functions.[19,20]

Sequencing Adaptive and Directive Leadership

Successful scale-up efforts rarely rely exclusively on either adaptive or directive leadership. Instead, they sequence these approaches over time. Directive leadership often dominates early phases of scale-up, when alignment and mobilization are paramount. Adaptive leadership becomes more prominent as interventions encounter contextual variation and require local problem-solving.

Dr. Tedros's leadership at WHO illustrates this sequencing. The early phases of WHO's Transformation Agenda, undertaken in support of GPW13, involved directive institutional reform, including restructuring and performance management. Over time, leadership emphasis shifted toward learning, data use, and country-level adaptation.[5] Similarly, Dilip Mahalanabis exemplified the deliberate sequencing of directive and adaptive leadership during large-scale cholera outbreaks.

In the acute phase of the crisis, he exercised directive leadership by organizing care delivery under extreme resource constraints, prioritizing triage, standardizing treatment protocols, and allocating scarce intravenous fluids to the most severely ill. As conditions evolved, including rapidly increasing patient volumes, shortages of trained medical staff, and the recognition that conventional hospital-based care models were insufficient, Mahalanabis adapted his leadership approach. He authorized the widespread use of oral rehydration therapy and deliberately expanded delivery beyond professional health workers to include paramedics, volunteers, and family members. This adaptive use of non-medical personnel reflected a pragmatic response to system overload, enabling rapid scale-up of life-saving treatment while maintaining clinical oversight and strategic coherence. By combining centralized coordination with flexible task shifting in response to contextual constraints, Mahalanabis demonstrated how leaders can preserve strategic intent while adapting operational models to evolving system realities.[21]

Hybrid leadership that intentionally sequences directive and adaptive approaches allows scale-up efforts to maintain coherence while responding effectively to complexity.

Balancing Innovation and Evidence-Based Practice

Fidelity, Adaptation, and Leadership Judgment

Scaling up requires balancing fidelity to evidence-based interventions with adaptation to new contexts. Excessive rigidity can undermine relevance and uptake, while excessive adaptation can erode effectiveness. Leadership plays a central role in navigating this tension by defining which elements of an intervention are essential and which can be modified. Figure 2.2 depicts leadership judgment as the mechanism that determines when evidence should standardize practice and when it should enable disciplined adaptation and innovation during scale-up, especially as interventions move across varied implementation contexts.

Implementation and scale-up research increasingly distinguishes between core functions and forms. Core functions represent the mechanisms through which an intervention achieves its effects. Forms represent the specific ways those

	Low Contextual Variability	High Contextual Variability
High Evidence Base	• Fidelity and standardization • Directive leadership • Examples: Surgical Safety Checklist, CDC Tips	• Protect core functions, adapt forms • Hybrid leadership • Examples: ORS, Ethiopia HSEP, Rwanda CBHI
Low Evidence Base	• Pilot and evaluate Adaptive leadership • Structured learning before scale • Examples: WHO GPW13 organizational reforms and delivery dashboards	• Adaptive experimentation • Rapid learning loops • Examples: Early COVID-19 response, Smallpox field strategies

Figure 2.2 Leadership Judgment in Balancing Fidelity and Adaptation

mechanisms are delivered. Leaders who protect core functions while allowing flexibility in forms are better positioned to achieve scale without sacrificing impact.[22]

Innovation as a Disciplined Response to Constraint

Innovation at scale often arises from necessity rather than novelty. Many influential global health innovations emerged as pragmatic responses to resource constraints and operational challenges. Leadership determines whether such innovations are tested, refined, and institutionalized.

The development and scale-up of oral rehydration therapy, delivered through Oral Rehydration Salts (ORS) illustrate this process. Faced with shortages of intravenous fluids during cholera outbreaks, Dr. Dilip Mahalanabis adapted existing scientific knowledge into a simple oral formulation that could be administered widely.[23] The intervention was tested in real-world conditions and later validated through rigorous evaluation. Over time, ORS became a cornerstone of diarrheal disease management globally, with large-scale evaluations demonstrating sustained impact.[24]

Similar dynamics are evident in smallpox eradication and in Côte d'Ivoire's COVID-19 response. For example, innovations such as ring vaccination and workforce redeployment were grounded in evidence and refined through practice.[10,25] Leadership ensured that innovation was coupled with learning rather than treated as a one-time workaround.

Evidence as Infrastructure for Scale

Evidence supports scale-up not only by demonstrating effectiveness but also by enabling governance and legitimacy. Robust data systems allow leaders to monitor progress, identify gaps, and justify continued investment. Evidence becomes infrastructure when it is institutionalized through measurement systems and feedback loops.

The Global Burden of Disease (GBD) study represents evidence as infrastructure. By standardizing metrics, incorporating uncertainty intervals, and enabling international comparison, GBD created a durable platform for health priority setting and accountability.[26,27] Similarly, WHO's investment in data platforms and delivery dashboards under GPW13 strengthened the organization's capacity to translate evidence into action.[28]

When Evidence Enables Innovation

Evidence does not merely constrain innovation. It can enable it by clarifying boundaries for experimentation. Leaders who understand the evidence base can identify where adaptation is necessary and where fidelity must be maintained. In Rwanda's community-based health insurance program, evidence from household surveys informed adaptive financing mechanisms while preserving the core function of risk pooling.[3,29] In Ethiopia's Health Extension Program, evidence on maternal and child health outcomes guided innovations in community mobilization and service delivery.[2,30]

In these cases, leadership used evidence not as a barrier to change but as a foundation for informed adaptation, allowing innovation to strengthen rather than undermine scale-up.

Leadership Moves

- **Anchor vision early, but design it to travel.** Effective leaders articulate a clear, equity-oriented vision at the outset of scale-up, but they resist over-specifying tactics too soon. Vision should define the destination and the values that guide trade-offs, while leaving room for adaptation as interventions encounter diverse institutional, political, and cultural contexts.
- **Translate vision into strategy that people can execute.** Vision becomes consequential only when it is operationalized into priorities, targets, and governance arrangements. Leaders must invest in strategic direction that clarifies decision rights, accountability, and sequencing, particularly as scale-up expands beyond pilot settings into national or multi-country systems.
- **Sequence directive and adaptive leadership deliberately.** Scale-up requires leaders to move fluidly between directive leadership, which provides alignment and momentum, and adaptive leadership, which enables learning and problem-solving. Early phases often demand clarity, authority, and coordination, while later phases require listening, negotiation, and contextual adjustment. Treating these approaches as complementary rather than competing is essential for sustained scale.
- **Protect core functions while allowing delivery forms to evolve.** Leaders play a critical role in distinguishing what must remain constant from what can change. Evidence should be used to identify the non-negotiable mechanisms

that drive impact, while innovation should be encouraged in how those mechanisms are delivered across settings. Over-standardization can undermine relevance, while uncontrolled adaptation can erode effectiveness.

- **Treat evidence as leadership infrastructure, not a technical add-on.** Data systems, monitoring frameworks, and feedback loops are not merely evaluation tools. They are core leadership assets that enable learning, legitimacy, and course correction at scale. Leaders who invest in evidence infrastructure strengthen their ability to govern complexity and sustain political and financial commitment.
- **Build legitimacy as intentionally as systems and services.** Trust, moral authority, and perceived fairness consistently shape whether scale-up efforts gain traction or face resistance. Leaders must engage communities, frontline workers, and institutional partners not only as implementers but as stakeholders whose buy-in determines long-term success.
- **Expect scale-up to reshape leadership itself.** As interventions expand, leadership demands evolve. What works in early expansion may undermine sustainability if not recalibrated. Effective leaders continuously reassess their role, shifting from champions of innovation to stewards of systems.

References

1. Damschroder LJ, Aron DC, Keith RE, Kirsh SR, Alexander JA, Lowery JC. Fostering implementation of health services research findings into practice: a consolidated framework for advancing implementation science. Implementation Sci. 2009 Aug 7;4(1):50.
2. Admasu KB. Designing a resilient national health system in Ethiopia: the role of leadership. Health Systems & Reform. 2016 Jul 2;2(3):182–6.
3. Lu C, Chin B, Lewandowski JL, Basinga P, Hirschhorn LR, Hill K, et al. Towards universal health coverage: an evaluation of Rwanda Mutuelles in its first eight years. PLOS ONE. 2012 Jun 18;7(6):e39282.
4. Transforming Healthcare in Rwanda with Agnes Binagwaho, MD, PhD [Internet]. (Explore Global Health with Rob Murphy, MD). Available from: https://www.globalhealth.northwestern.edu/events/podcast/binagwaho.html
5. Lange JE. Aligning for impact: the transformation of the World Health Organization [Internet]. United Nations Foundation; 2019 [cited 2026 Feb 17]. Available from: https://unfoundation.org/blog/post/aligning-for-impact-the-transformation-of-the-world-health-organization/
6. World Bank Group. Cote d'Ivoire – COVID-19 Strategic Preparedness and Response Project [Internet]. Washington, DC: World Bank Group; 2022 Apr [cited 2026 Jan 10]. Available from: http://documents.worldbank.org/curated/en/876821649959319200
7. Samuel K, Palazuelos D. Nonprofit leadership lessons from Dr. Paul Farmer (SSIR) [Internet]. Stanford Social Innovation Review; 2022 [cited 2026 Feb 17]. Available from: https://ssir.org/articles/entry/nonprofit_leadership_lessons_from_dr_paul_farmer
8. Partners in Health Canada. How Dr. Paul Farmer Revolutionized Tuberculosis Care [Internet]. 2024 [cited 2026 Jan 6]. Available from: https://pihcanada.org/news/how-dr-paul-farmer-revolutionized-tuberculosis-care
9. Schindler H, Wallen M, Schindler H, Wallen M. Paul Farmer: a pioneer of global health, health equity, and health advocacy. Cureus [Internet]. 2024 Oct 2 [cited 2026 Jan 10];16.

Available from: https://cureus.com/articles/291043-paul-farmer-a-pioneer-of-global-health-health-equity-and-health-advocacy
10. Foege W. House on fire: the fight to eradicate smallpox. Oakland, CA: University of California Press; 2011. 240 p.
11. Heifetz RA, Grashow A, Linsky M. The practice of adaptive leadership: tools and tactics for changing your organization and the world. Brighton, MA: Harvard Business Press; 2009. 352 p.
12. World Bank Group. COVID-19 vaccines: from rejection to shortage, how Côte d'Ivoire became a model for managing vaccine hesitancy [Internet]. 2021 [cited 2026 Jan 18]. Available from: https://www.worldbank.org/en/news/feature/2021/09/07/covid-19-vaccines-from-rejection-to-shortage-how-c-te-d-ivoire-became-a-model-for-managing-vaccine-hesitancy
13. Murphy-Hoefer R, Davis KC, King BA, Beistle D, Rodes R, Graffunder C. Association between the tips from former smokers campaign and smoking cessation among adults, United States, 2012–2018. Prev Chronic Dis. 2020 Aug 27;17:E97.
14. CDC. Newsroom – tips from former smokers [Internet]. Centers for Disease Control and Prevention; 2024. Available from: https://www.cdc.gov/tobacco/campaign/tips/press/index.html
15. CDC. Frequently asked questions about the tips campaign [Internet]. Centers for Disease Control and Prevention; 2024 [cited 2026 Jan 10]. Available from: https://www.cdc.gov/tobacco/campaign/tips/about/faq/campaign-faq.html
16. Rosenburg J, Ahmad I, Weintraub R. Eradicating smallpox: delivery strategies to reach the last mile [Internet]. Harvard Medical School; 2022 [cited 2026 Jan 10]. Available from: https://hsph.harvard.edu/wp-content/uploads/2025/10/ghd-047_smallpox_updated.pdf
17. Walker IA, Reshamwalla S, Wilson IH. Surgical safety checklists: do they improve outcomes? British Journal of Anaesthesia. 2012 Jul 1;109(1):47–54.
18. Keegan MJ. Leadership insights from "The Checklist Manifesto: How to Get Things Right" [Internet]. IBM Center for The Business of Government; 2024 [cited 2026 Jan 10]. Available from: https://www.businessofgovernment.org/blog/leadership-insights-checklist-manifesto-how-get-things-right
19. Integrated Health Services. Patient safety: safe surgery saves lives [Internet]. World Health Organization; 2014 [cited 2026 Jan 10]. Available from: https://www.who.int/news-room/questions-and-answers/item/safe-surgery-saves-lives-frequently-asked-questions
20. NHS England. Decade of improved outcomes for patients thanks to Surgical Safety Checklist [Internet]. 2019 [cited 2026 Jan 10]. Available from: https://www.england.nhs.uk/2019/01/surgical-safety-checklist/
21. Kawalkar U, Mankar A, Kogade P, Naitam D. Dr. Dilip Mahalanabis (1934–2022): trailblazer in diarrheal disease management. Cureus. 2024 Jun;16(6):e62241.
22. Greenhalgh T, Wherton J, Papoutsi C, Lynch J, Hughes G, A'Court C, et al. Beyond adoption: a new framework for theorizing and evaluating nonadoption, abandonment, and challenges to the scale-up, spread, and sustainability of health and care technologies. Journal of Medical Internet Research. 2017 Nov 1;19(11):e8775.
23. Chatterjee R, Chandra A, George A, Dasgupta S. Oral rehydration solution: a landmark discovery in medicine and the legacy of Dr. Dilip Mahalanabis. The American Journal of Medicine. 2025 Mar 1;138(3):384–6.
24. Lam F, Abdulwahab A, Houdek J, Adekeye O, Abubakar M, Akinjeji A, et al. Program evaluation of an ORS and zinc scale-up program in 8 Nigerian states. Journal of Global Health. 2019 Jun;9(1):010502.

25. World Health Organization Cote D'Ivoire. Expanding COVID-19 vaccination in Cote d'Ivoire [Internet]. 2022 [cited 2026 Feb 17]. Available from: https://www.afro.who.int/countries/cote-divoire/news/expanding-covid-19-vaccination-cote-divoire
26. Murray CJL, Lopez AD. Measuring the global burden of disease. New England Journal of Medicine. 2013 Aug 1;369(5):448–57.
27. Institute for Health Metrics and Evaluation. The global burden of disease: generating evidence, guiding policy [Internet]. Seattle, Washington: Institute for Health Metrics and Evaluation; 2013 p. 28. Available from: https://www.healthdata.org/research-analysis/library/global-burden-disease-generating-evidence-guiding-policy
28. World Health Organization. Evaluation of the Thirteenth General Programme of Work [Internet]. 2025. Available from: https://www.who.int/publications/i/item/9789240095090
29. Musabwasoni SMG, Oudshoorn A. Considering healthcare insurance to uninsured individuals in Rwanda. Rwanda Journal of Medicine and Health Sciences. 2019 Mar 25;2(1):59–61.
30. Karim AM, Admassu K, Schellenberg J, Alemu H, Getachew N, Ameha A, et al. Effect of Ethiopia's health extension program on maternal and newborn health care practices in 101 rural districts: a dose-response study. PLOS ONE. 2013 Jun 4;8(6):e65160.

3 Aligning Systems for Sustainable Scale

Scale as a Systems Challenge

Scaling up health interventions is often described as a matter of expansion: reaching more people, replicating what worked in a pilot, and increasing service coverage across districts or countries. Yet the historical record of global health demonstrates that scale-up is rarely constrained by the intervention alone. The dominant constraints are systemic. As interventions grow, they must operate through health systems composed of interacting parts: workforces, service delivery platforms, information systems, procurement and supply chains, financing arrangements, governance structures, and policy environments. These parts do not function independently. They interact dynamically, creating feedback loops that can reinforce success or amplify failure. A systems perspective therefore reframes scale-up from a technical problem of replication to a complex problem of alignment.

A systems perspective emphasizes interdependence, nonlinearity, and adaptation. Rather than assuming that an intervention will produce the same outcome wherever it is implemented, systems thinking asks how context shapes mechanisms, how relationships among actors and institutions enable or block implementation, and how interventions alter the systems they enter. These insights matter because large-scale implementation changes the very conditions under which it occurs. Growth increases heterogeneity, creates new coordination demands, and raises the stakes of policy choices. Scale-up therefore becomes as much a governance challenge as a technical one, particularly when interventions evolve into broader system-level innovations.

This chapter argues that sustainable scale-up requires three system-level conditions. First, health system components must be deliberately strengthened and aligned to support expansion. Scale-up depends on the availability and distribution of the workforce, the reliability of service delivery platforms, the functioning of information systems, access to medicines and technologies, and the sustainability of financing mechanisms.[1,2] Second, scale-up is inherently multi-sectoral. Governments, non-governmental organizations (NGOs), the private sector, and communities each hold distinct capacities and forms of authority, and scale requires structured collaboration among these actors rather than ad hoc partnership.[3,4] Third, enabling policy and regulatory frameworks convert collaboration and system

DOI: 10.4324/9781003685821-5

capacity into durable institutional practice by stabilizing roles, incentives, and accountability mechanisms.[5,6] Together, these conditions clarify why some interventions move from demonstration to institutionalized scale, while others remain fragmented or fragile.

The chapter proceeds in three sections. The first examines how health system components enable or constrain scale-up, focusing on workforce, service delivery, information systems, medicines and technologies, financing, and governance. The second examines multi-sectoral collaboration, showing how coordinated action across government, NGOs, private providers, and community structures produces scale in diverse contexts, including immunization, health insurance, HIV care, and integrated community programs. The third examines the policy and regulatory frameworks that stabilize scale by shaping incentives, institutional authority, and accountability.

Across these sections, the central claim is that scale is less a matter of "scaling interventions" and more a matter of aligning systems. Table 3.1 synthesizes the system components, actors, and policy conditions that must align for health interventions to scale sustainably, highlighting where scale most commonly breaks down—and where leadership and governance interventions are most consequential. Read diagnostically, the table underscores a recurring pattern: scale most often fails not at the point of innovation, but where system components, actors, and policies fall out of alignment.

The Role of Health Systems in Scaling Interventions

Health Systems as Active Enablers or Constraints

A common mistake in scale-up is treating health systems as neutral platforms that will simply "carry" an intervention once funding and training are provided. In reality, health systems are active determinants of implementation success. They govern how resources flow, decisions are made, frontline workers behave, and communities experience services. Even when an intervention has strong evidence, it will not scale if the system cannot absorb it. Conversely, interventions with modest technical sophistication can scale rapidly when they align with system incentives and routines.

A systems approach highlights that barriers to scale often appear in predictable places. Workforce constraints are among the most visible. Global health continues to face a human resources crisis, marked by shortages, uneven distribution, weak incentives, and limited supervisory capacity.[1,2] These constraints are not merely logistical; they shape the equity profile of scale-up. When skilled providers cluster in urban centers, rural and marginalized communities receive less consistent services even when national coverage expands. Systems thinking therefore requires leaders to focus not only on expanding services but on shaping system capacity and distributional equity.

Equally important is recognizing that strengthening one system component can create pressure elsewhere. Expanding community-based primary care increases

Table 3.1 System Components, Actors, and Policy Conditions for Health Intervention Scale-Up

System Component	*Primary Function in Scale-Up*	*Key Actors Involved*	*Typical Failure Mode at Scale*	*Enabling Policy or Governance Condition*
Health workforce	Delivers services consistently and equitably at scale	Ministry of Health, training institutions, professional councils, NGOs, community structures, frontline workers	Workforce shortages, uneven geographic distribution, burnout, weak supervision	National workforce strategies, task-shifting regulations, standardized training and supervision policies
Service delivery platforms	Provide accessible, reliable points of care across populations	Government providers, NGOs, private clinics, community-based organizations	Fragmentation, variable quality, weak referral linkages	Service delivery standards, contracting frameworks, accreditation and quality assurance mechanisms
Health information systems	Enable monitoring, learning, and accountability during expansion	Ministries of Health, district authorities, implementing partners, donors	Incomplete or delayed reporting, poor data use, weak feedback loops	Mandatory reporting policies, investment in digital infrastructure, data governance and use protocols
Medicines and technologies	Ensure availability and quality of essential inputs at scale	Government procurement agencies, private suppliers, donors, regulators	Stock-outs, supply-chain bottlenecks, inequitable access, quality lapses	Essential Medicines Lists, procurement and pricing regulations, cold-chain and quality-control standards
Financing mechanisms	Sustain service utilization and protect equity as coverage expands	Ministries of Finance, insurers, donors, households	High out-of-pocket payments, unstable funding, adverse selection	Health financing laws, pooled insurance schemes, subsidy and purchasing policies
Governance and coordination	Align actors, manage trade-offs, and sustain accountability	Government stewardship bodies, NGOs, private sector, civil society	Duplication, power struggles, weak accountability, dependence on individuals	Clear stewardship authority, intersectoral coordination mechanisms, performance monitoring frameworks

demand for medicines, referrals, laboratory services, and data reporting. If supply chains remain weak, stock-outs undermine trust. If referral systems cannot handle increased volume, frontline providers lose legitimacy. If data systems do not improve, leaders cannot see gaps in performance. Scale-up therefore requires coordinated strengthening across system components rather than isolated interventions.

Health Workforce: Designing for Reach and Continuity

Frontline workers are the practical engine of scale-up, particularly in settings where facility-based care cannot reach dispersed populations. The global evidence base consistently shows that task-shifting and community health worker programs can extend services into underserved areas when they are properly supported and embedded within systems.[7] The critical issue is not whether community-based workers exist, but whether they are trained, supervised, incentivized, and integrated into formal health structures.

Ethiopia's Health Extension Worker program illustrates how workforce strategy can enable scale. The program expanded rural coverage by deploying trained workers into communities, creating a platform for maternal and child health services and prevention-oriented primary care.[8] Evidence suggests expansion contributed to improved coverage and equity in service delivery. The broader implication is that scaling is not achieved through workforce numbers alone, but through the institutional design of training, supervisory routines, and system integration.

The system-level lesson is that workforce expansion alone does not produce sustainable scale. Persistent shortages and uneven distribution can reproduce inequities even as national coverage indicators improve.[2] When incentives are weak and supervision is inconsistent, expanded reach translates into variable performance and attrition rather than durable capacity. Systems thinking reframes workforce policy as an integrative design problem: training, deployment, financing, supply chain reliability, and information systems must advance together. When these elements are misaligned, scale-up generates implementation fatigue and quality erosion instead of resilience over time. Yet even a well-designed workforce cannot deliver scale on its own; the impact of human resources ultimately depends on the service delivery platforms through which care is organized and reaches communities.

Service Delivery Platforms: Scaling Through Community-Based Structures

Service delivery platforms determine how interventions reach people. Many successful scale-up efforts rely on community-based service delivery rather than facilities alone, especially where geography and poverty create barriers to care. Pakistan's Lady Health Worker Programme offers a widely cited example of scaling primary care through structured community delivery. Each worker served a defined number of households, provided doorstep services, followed standardized training curricula, and received supervisory visits.[9] These features created a repeatable service platform capable of reaching a large proportion of the population.

The broader lesson is that scale requires platform design: clear catchment definitions, standardized service packages, supervisory routines, and institutional accountability. Community delivery is not simply decentralization; it is system architecture. Yet the Pakistan case also demonstrates that scaling platforms can reveal weaknesses in other system components. Initial supply stock-outs and variations in supervisory quality across districts constrained performance.[9] This illustrates a recurring systems pattern: expanding delivery without strengthening supply chains and supervision produces uneven outcomes.

From a systems perspective, service platforms also mediate trust. Doorstep care can strengthen relationships between health systems and communities, but only when service reliability is maintained. When stock-outs occur or referrals fail, community trust declines, reducing uptake and compromising sustainability. Scale-up thus requires leaders to think beyond service coverage and attend to the relational and infrastructural conditions that keep platforms credible.

Information Systems: Making Performance Visible and Actionable

While service platforms shape how care is experienced on the ground, information systems determine whether those experiences are visible, comparable, and governable at scale. Information systems determine whether scale-up is governable or blind. Without reliable data, leaders cannot see where coverage is lagging, where equity gaps persist, or which implementation strategies are failing. Systems thinking emphasizes that measurement is not an add-on; it is a form of infrastructure that shapes system behavior.

For example, Ghana's experience with electronic surveillance and reporting platforms illustrates the potential reminders and digital infrastructure can have for routine reporting. Improvements in completeness and timeliness were documented following roll-out of an internet-based platform, mobile phone reminders, and training of district officers.[10] These improvements are meaningful because they strengthen the feedback loops that allow systems to respond to outbreaks, allocate resources, and adjust program delivery. The lesson is that digital platforms enable scale when they are designed for routine use and supported by training and organizational capacity.

At the same time, information systems often remain fragile at the periphery. Reliance on paper-based reporting, transmission errors, and uneven adoption across levels undermine data reliability. Systems thinking therefore emphasizes that data systems require institutional routines: supervision, incentives for reporting, and local capacity to interpret and act on data. Scaling information systems is not purely technical; it is organizational and political.[10]

Access to Essential Medicines: Procurement, Affordability, and Reliability

Scale-up fails quickly when essential medicines are unavailable or unaffordable. Access to medicines depends on procurement policies, supply chain coordination, financing reliability, and market regulation. Evidence from multi-country surveys demonstrates that medicine availability in public sectors can be strikingly low, even for basic generics, and that affordability remains a persistent barrier.[11] These findings underscore that the ability to deliver interventions at scale is constrained by system capacity to procure and distribute medicines reliably.

Procurement strategies such as centralized tendering for generics, adoption of essential medicines lists, and monitoring of price ratios can support scale by reducing costs and improving consistency. Yet fragmentation, inadequate financing, and weak supply chain governance remain common barriers.[11] From a systems perspective, the key point is that medicine access is not a discrete technical issue; it is a system function that determines whether service platforms remain trustworthy and effective.

When medicine availability is low, providers may ration care, communities may seek unregulated alternatives, and program outcomes may deteriorate. These dynamics create reinforcing feedback loops that undermine scale. Systems thinking thus requires leaders to treat procurement and supply chain management as core determinants of intervention success, not administrative back-office functions.

Vaccines and Technologies: Cold-Chain Systems as Scaling Infrastructure

Vaccines and health technologies require specialized distribution infrastructure. Cold-chain capacity is not a peripheral technical requirement; it is a central scaling constraint in immunization programs and outbreak responses. Evidence from assessments of cold-chain management in Nigeria highlights both achievements and vulnerabilities: vaccines can remain within expected potency margins, yet system weaknesses persist, including equipment lapses, power interruptions, and training gaps in cold-chain monitoring.[12]

These findings illustrate a systems insight: scale depends on reliability. Cold-chain systems require stable power, equipment maintenance, trained personnel, and monitoring routines. When any component fails, the entire system becomes fragile. Scaling immunization therefore requires strengthening infrastructure, supervision, and accountability. Systems thinking shifts the focus from vaccine supply alone to the organizational and infrastructural systems that make vaccines usable.

Technology scale-up also raises equity issues. Central facilities may be well equipped, while peripheral facilities face shortages and weak monitoring. Without deliberate attention, scale can widen gaps between regions. Leaders therefore need to treat technology delivery as a system-wide design problem, incorporating redundancy, maintenance capacity, and training into scale strategies.

Financing: Pooling Risk and Stabilizing Access

Financing is often framed as a question of resource availability. Systems thinking emphasizes that financing is also a question of structure: how funds are mobilized, pooled, allocated, and protected from volatility. Community-based health insurance models offer insights into how risk pooling can improve access and reduce catastrophic spending, thereby enabling sustained service utilization at scale.[13,14]

Rwanda's Mutuelles de Santé is frequently cited as a strong example of scaling insurance coverage through community-based risk pooling, premium subsidies, and integration with national policy objectives. Evidence suggests that the scheme increased utilization and offered protection against catastrophic spending.[13,14] Importantly, systems thinking highlights that financing reforms succeed when they are embedded within governance arrangements that manage adverse selection, enforce contributions, and ensure quality of care.

Barriers remain common across contexts: low public expenditure, high out-of-pocket payments, and adverse selection undermine sustainability.[13,14] Scale-up strategies must therefore consider the political economy of health financing, including public trust, government fiscal capacity, and the administrative infrastructure needed to manage enrollment and claims.

Governance: Coordination, Accountability, and System Learning

Finally, governance shapes scale by determining how decisions are made, how accountability is enforced, and how local adaptation is managed. Brazil's Family Health Program illustrates how decentralized municipal management combined with performance monitoring can produce measurable population health outcomes. Evidence indicates that increased program coverage was associated with reductions in infant mortality, suggesting that governance design can enable sustained improvements at scale.[15,16]

From a systems perspective, governance is not simply oversight. It is the mechanism through which systems learn and adjust. When local management capacity is variable or politically interfered with, program performance becomes inconsistent.[15,16] Effective governance therefore requires a balance: enough decentralization to enable responsiveness, and enough central stewardship to ensure equity and standardization where needed.

Taken together, these cases show that health systems do not merely support scale-up; they actively shape its pace, equity, and durability. Scale succeeds not when systems are bypassed, but when they are deliberately designed to absorb, adapt, and sustain interventions and the broader innovations they generate.

Engaging Governments, NGOs, and the Private Sector

Scale-Up as Multi-Sectoral Work

Scale-up requires multiple forms of power and capacity. Governments hold regulatory authority and can stabilize financing and institutionalization. NGOs often introduce delivery innovations, mobilize community trust, and provide adaptive capacity that formal systems struggle to sustain. The private sector shapes supply chains, service delivery markets, and technology deployment. Communities determine uptake, legitimacy, and sustained engagement. Systems thinking emphasizes that these actors form a network, not a hierarchy, and scale depends on the quality of coordination across that network.

Multi-sectoral coordination is often described as stakeholder engagement, yet engagement and social mobilization are not interchangeable. Stakeholder engagement aligns institutional actors who control resources, rules, and delivery platforms. Social mobilization activates communities as participants in implementation, shaping trust, uptake, and sustained adherence in ways formal authority alone cannot secure. Scale can advance through elite coordination while faltering at the last mile if communities are not meaningfully involved. Engagement stabilizes roles and agreements; mobilization stabilizes legitimacy and behavioral adoption. Durable scale requires both.

The polio eradication experience in India illustrates how multi-sectoral coordination can achieve extraordinary scale. Coordinated action among government institutions, international organizations, and community leaders enabled joint planning and synchronized delivery strategies.[3] Community mobilization and micro-planning were critical, reflecting the reality that technical solutions alone do not reach the last mile. The achievement of near-total eradication depended not only on vaccine effectiveness but on collaboration structures capable of sustaining repeated campaigns and rapid response to surveillance data.[3,17]

Systems thinking also highlights that multi-sectoral collaboration is costly. It requires time, negotiation, and governance arrangements that clarify roles and prevent duplication. Without structure, multi-sectoral efforts can become fragmented. When successful, they become a form of system capacity that endures beyond one intervention, creating a platform for future responses.

Government Stewardship and Policy Authority

Government stewardship is central to enhancing system capacity because governments can set national priorities, standardize guidelines, and institutionalize programs. In universal health coverage reforms, government authority is essential for pooling risk, defining benefits, and regulating provider payment. Mexico's reform illustrates how a government-led approach can mobilize financing and standardize a benefits package at scale.[4] However, the system-level effect depends on whether reforms translate into equitable access and whether community engagement is integrated into delivery.

Evidence indicates that coverage expansions may benefit marginalized groups when outreach and design are intentional. For example, analyses of utilization among Indigenous populations suggest that insurance reforms can increase access in socially inequitable contexts when combined with supportive implementation and community engagement.[18] These findings highlight an important systems insight: policy reform must be accompanied by delivery and trust-building mechanisms, otherwise formal coverage does not translate into real access.

Government stewardship is also critical in outbreak response. National targets, standardized reporting requirements, and coordinated deployment can accelerate scale. Without government leadership, donor-funded programs may scale temporarily but fail to institutionalize. Systems thinking therefore frames government not as a partner among equals, but as a steward responsible for aligning the system and protecting equity.

NGOs as Innovation and Trust Brokers

In addition to government stewardships, NGOs often provide capacities that health systems struggle to sustain, including community engagement, rapid adaptation, and integrated social support. In Bangladesh, the Bangladesh Rehabilitation Assistance Committee (BRAC)'s model links microfinance with health education, demonstrating how NGO platforms can expand health knowledge and influence health outcomes when embedded in community structures.[19] Evidence suggests that participation in integrated programs is associated with higher health knowledge and improved child outcomes over time, illustrating how non-state delivery platforms can complement formal services.[19,20]

From a systems perspective, NGOs can function as trust brokers and innovators, but scale depends on alignment with public systems. When NGO programs remain parallel, sustainability risks increase. Regulatory frameworks that clarify NGO roles can therefore facilitate scale by stabilizing operations and enabling collaboration with government systems. Systems thinking encourages leaders to treat NGO platforms as assets to be integrated, not substitutes that bypass state capacity.

The Private Sector: Supply Chains, Providers, and Platforms

Whereas NGOs typically support scale-up through programmatic delivery, community engagement, and policy advocacy within public systems, the private sector influences scale primarily through market mechanisms that shape the availability, distribution, and delivery of health technologies and services. The private sector shapes scale-up through medicine and vaccine markets, logistics, and service delivery. Private providers often fill gaps in public services, and private logistics networks can support cold chain and distribution. Yet private sector involvement can also introduce risks: inequitable access, variable quality, and profit-driven incentives that conflict with public goals. Systems thinking emphasizes that the private sector can enable scale, but only when regulation and contracting align incentives with equity.

In health insurance reforms and subsidized schemes, private hospitals and providers can expand service availability, but they also require accountability mechanisms to prevent overbilling and ensure quality. In HIV scale-up, private clinics can extend reach, but adherence and follow-up may depend on community networks. The key point is that private sector involvement must be governed, not assumed.

Case Logic: HIV Scale-Up as Structured Collaboration

HIV scale-up provides a clear demonstration of multi-sectoral collaboration as system design. In Uganda, the expansion of antiretroviral therapy was supported by external funding, government stewardship of clinical guidelines, NGO-led community support, and delivery through public and private facilities. Evidence suggests rapid increases in coverage over time and improvements in outcomes among recipients when treatment programs are sustained and monitored.[21]

Two systems insights follow. First, scale depends on coordination: procurement, guideline dissemination, clinician training, and community support must align. Second, scale depends on institutionalization: as programs expand, governance and accountability mechanisms must stabilize to prevent quality decline and inequity. Systems thinking frames HIV scale-up as a case of network governance, not merely program delivery.

Similarly, Kenya's AMPATH network demonstrates how academic institutions can provide technical leadership while governments integrate services and NGOs manage clinics and community engagement. Evidence suggests large patient volumes and retention outcomes when decentralized hubs and adherence support are maintained.[5,22] These cases illustrate that successful collaboration builds durable networks that can adapt over time while preserving core functions.

Policy and Regulatory Frameworks That Enable Scale

Policy as the Architecture of Scale

Policy is often treated as context. In scale-up, policy is architecture. It defines what is funded, what is permitted, who is responsible, and what accountability exists. Supportive policies can enable coordination, stabilize financing, and institutionalize delivery platforms. Weak or ambiguous policies can fragment efforts and discourage investment. Systems thinking thus treats policy as a lever that can reshape system behavior.

Policy also determines whether ownership becomes institutional rather than temporary. Many interventions expand through externally led delivery arrangements that accelerate coverage but leave core system functions—including financing, supervision, procurement, and reporting—anchored outside domestic institutions. Without a deliberate transition pathway, such arrangements generate scale without institutional absorption. When donor timelines substitute for domestic accountability, sustainability becomes fragile. Durable scale therefore requires leadership to design for ownership from the outset, specifying how authority, resources, and performance management will shift over time to government and community actors while protecting quality and equity during that transfer.

India's polio eradication experience illustrates how policy decisions can enable synchronized mass campaigns by legitimizing national immunization days and strengthening surveillance and reporting requirements.[3] Policy enabled coordination across states and organizations, and it created an expectation of repeated campaigns and rapid response. Importantly, systems thinking emphasizes that policy works through institutions: reporting laws matter when information systems can produce timely data and when local authorities act on it.

In health financing reforms, policy determines whether coverage becomes real access. Mexico's reform was not simply a financing decision; it was a legal and institutional redesign that mandated benefit expansion and clarified responsibilities across levels of government.[4] Evidence that utilization increased and coverage expanded among marginalized groups underscores that policy can reshape incentives, but only when implementation structures support delivery.[18]

Regulation: Enabling Flexibility While Protecting Standards

Regulatory frameworks shape scale by establishing standards for quality, safety, and accountability. Yet scale requires flexibility. Systems thinking highlights the tension: standardization enables coordination, but rigidity undermines responsiveness. Policies that enable local adaptation while protecting core functions are more likely to succeed.

In social health insurance, regulation determines provider payment, benefit packages, enrollment rules, and grievance mechanisms. The Philippines' reforms and evaluations of financing changes suggest that removing user fees can increase utilization rapidly and reduce catastrophic spending, but sustaining those gains depends on provider capacity and financing reliability.[5,6] Systems thinking interprets such reforms as changes in system incentives: when financial barriers fall, demand increases; if supply capacity does not expand, quality may decline. Regulation must therefore anticipate system feedback effects.

In NGO-supported programs, regulation can either impede or enable integrated models. Bangladesh's experience with NGO regulation suggests that institutional rules can stabilize operations and allow long-term integration of programs that combine social and health interventions.[19,20] The lesson is that regulation is not only constraint; it can be a platform for collaboration when it clarifies roles and supports accountability.

Institutionalization: Moving from Program to Routine Practice

Policy adoption is not the endpoint; institutionalization is. Scale-up becomes durable when it is embedded in budgets, staffing structures, information systems, procurement routines, and accountability mechanisms. Systems thinking emphasizes that sustainability emerges when interventions become "normal" within system routines.

Health workforce platforms become durable when they are formally incorporated into public service structures, with stable remuneration and supervision.[7] Data systems become durable when reporting routines are required, resourced, and used for decision-making.[10] Insurance schemes become durable when financing is stabilized, risk pooling is maintained, and providers are accountable for quality.[13,14] Governance reforms become durable when performance monitoring persists across political cycles and local capacity is supported.[15,16]

A final systems insight concerns equity. Scale-up can expand national averages while leaving marginalized communities behind. Policy and regulation therefore must explicitly address distribution: workforce deployment rules, subsidy design, benefit packages, and accountability for underserved regions. Systems thinking does not treat equity as an add-on; it treats equity as an emergent property of system design.

Leadership Moves

Leadership in sustainable scale begins with system alignment. The following moves help leaders strengthen the conditions that allow interventions to expand without fragmenting, exhausting, or bypassing the systems meant to sustain them.

- **Treat the health system as the unit of change.** Effective scale-up is achieved by strengthening and aligning the workforce, service delivery platforms, information systems, procurement and supply chains, financing mechanisms, and governance structures, not by expanding an intervention in isolation.
- **Design platforms for reliability before pursuing expansion.** Community-based delivery and task-shifting can expand reach, but scale becomes credible only when supply chains, supervision, and referral pathways are strong enough to prevent stock-outs, quality erosion, and loss of trust.
- **Use data systems to create learning loops.** Timely and complete reporting is not simply monitoring; it is the feedback infrastructure that enables course correction, equitable targeting, and rapid response as scale introduces heterogeneity.
- **Build structured collaboration across sectors.** Governments, NGOs, private providers, and communities hold distinct capacities. Scale depends on clear roles, aligned incentives, and shared accountability mechanisms that reduce duplication and sustain coordination.
- **Make policy and regulation work for implementation.** Policies that mandate coverage, define entitlements, and clarify institutional responsibilities stabilize scale. Regulation should protect quality and accountability while permitting local adaptation as systems learn.
- **Institutionalize what works by embedding it in routines.** The transition from program to system occurs when financing is stabilized, staffing and supervision are formalized, procurement is reliable, data systems are used, and governance is maintained across political cycles.

References

1. Health Workforce (HWF). The world health report 2006: working together for health [Internet]. Geneva: World Health Organization; 2006 Oct. p. 237. Available from: https://iris.who.int/server/api/core/bitstreams/f9e49704-ee93-4ed9-a66e-1f23791ddf89/content
2. Chen L, Evans T, Anand S, Boufford JI, Brown H, Chowdhury M, et al. Human resources for health: overcoming the crisis. Lancet. 2004 Dec 27;364(9449):1984–90.
3. Thacker N, Vashishtha VM, Thacker D. Polio eradication in India: the lessons learned. Pediatrics. 2016 Oct 1;138(4):e20160461.
4. Frenk J, González-Pier E, Gómez-Dantés O, Lezana MA, Knaul FM. Comprehensive reform to improve health system performance in Mexico. The Lancet. 2006 Oct 28;368(9546):1524–34.
5. Wools-Kaloustian KK, Sidle JE, Selke HM, Vedanthan R, Kemboi EK, Boit LJ, et al. A model for extending antiretroviral care beyond the rural health centre. JIAS. 2009 Sep 29;12(1):22.
6. Lagarde M, Palmer N. The impact of user fees on access to health services in low- and middle-income countries. Cochrane Database Syst Rev. 2011 Apr 13;2011(4):CD009094.

7. Health Workforce (HWF). What do we know about community health workers? A systematic review of existing reviews [Internet]. Geneva: World Health Organization; 2021 Apr p. 88. (Human Resources for Health Observer Series). Available from: https://www.who.int/publications/i/item/what-do-we-know-about-community-health-workers-a-systematic-review-of-existing-reviews
8. Workie NW, Ramana GN. The Health Extension Program in Ethiopia [Internet]. World Bank; 2013. (UNICO Studies Series). Available from: https://hdl.handle.net/10986/13280
9. Global Health Workforce Alliance Task Force on Scaling Up Education and Training for Health Workers. Country case study Pakistan's lady health worker programme [Internet]. World Health Organization; 2008. Available from: https://cewh.ca/wp-content/uploads/2019/09/untitled.pdf
10. Adokiya MN, Awoonor-Williams JK, Beiersmann C, Müller O. Evaluation of the reporting completeness and timeliness of the integrated disease surveillance and response system in northern Ghana. Ghana Med J. 2016 Mar;50(1):3–8.
11. Cameron A, Ewen M, Ross-Degnan D, Ball D, Laing R. Medicine prices, availability, and affordability in 36 developing and middle-income countries: a secondary analysis. The Lancet. 2009 Jan 17;373(9659):240–9.
12. Babatunde OA, Olatunji MB, Omotajo OR, Ikwunne OI, Hamzat Z, Sola ST. A comparative assessment of cold chain management using the outbreak of circulating vaccine-derived polio virus type 2 as a surrogate marker in Oyo State, Nigeria-2019. The Pan African Medical Journal [Internet]. 2020 Dec 3 [cited 2026 Jan 11];37(313). Available from: https://www.panafrican-med-journal.com//content/article/37/313/full
13. Saksena P, Antunes AF, Xu K, Musango L, Carrin G. Mutual health insurance in Rwanda: evidence on access to care and financial risk protection. Health Policy. 2011 Mar;99(3):203–9.
14. Lu C, Chin B, Lewandowski JL, Basinga P, Hirschhorn LR, Hill K, et al. Towards universal health coverage: an evaluation of Rwanda Mutuelles in its first eight years. PLOS ONE. 2012 Jun 18;7(6):e39282.
15. Macinko J, Guanais FC, Souza M de FM de. Evaluation of the impact of the Family Health Program on infant mortality in Brazil, 1990–2002. Journal of Epidemiology & Community Health. 2006 Jan 1;60(1):13–9.
16. Aquino R, de Oliveira NF, Barreto ML. Impact of the family health program on infant mortality in Brazilian municipalities. Am J Public Health. 2009 Jan;99(1):87–93.
17. Grassly NC, Wenger J, Durrani S, Bahl S, Deshpande JM, Sutter RW, et al. Protective efficacy of a monovalent oral type 1 poliovirus vaccine: a case-control study. The Lancet. 2007 Apr 21;369(9570):1356–62.
18. Leyva-Flores R, Servan-Mori E, Infante-Xibille C, Pelcastre-Villafuerte BE, Gonzalez T. Primary health care utilization by the Mexican Indigenous population: the role of the Seguro Popular in socially inequitable contexts. PLOS ONE. 2014 Aug 6;9(8):e102781.
19. Hadi A. Promoting health knowledge through micro-credit programmes: experience of BRAC in Bangladesh. Health Promot Int. 2001 Sep 1;16(3):219–27.
20. Leatherman S, Metcalfe M, Geissler K, Dunford C. Integrating microfinance and health strategies: examining the evidence to inform policy and practice. Health Policy Plan. 2012 Mar;27(2):85–101.
21. United States President's Emergency Plan For Aids Relief. Uganda Country/Regional Operational Plan 2016 Strategic Direction Summary [Internet]. United States Department of State; 2017. Available from: https://www.state.gov/wp-content/uploads/2019/08/Uganda-15.pdf
22. Rosen S, Fox MP, Gill CJ. Patient retention in antiretroviral therapy programs in sub-Saharan Africa: a systematic review. PLOS Medicine. 2007 Oct 16;4(10):e298.

Part II

Leadership Under Constraint

Part II examines leadership at scale through five comparative cases that illuminate distinct but recurring structural challenges in global health implementation. These chapters do not treat scale as expansion alone. They focus on the leadership judgment required when authority is fragmented, systems are uneven, and performance depends on actors who cannot be commanded into alignment. Each case isolates a different configuration of constraint, revealing how leadership operates under pressure rather than in ideal conditions.

Smallpox eradication illustrates the problem of coordinating sovereign actors without centralized enforcement authority. Malaria bed net scale-up demonstrates the difficulty of sustaining protection when effectiveness depends on behavior beyond formal command and when implementation strain accumulates over time. The elimination of epidemic meningitis reveals the necessity of adapting interventions to structural limits rather than waiting for systems to meet idealized standards. Ethiopia's Health Extension Program highlights the orchestration required in decentralized systems where legitimacy and coordination must be constructed simultaneously. COVID-19 vaccine scale-up exposes the tension between speed and legitimacy when urgency collides with evolving evidence and contested trust.

Taken together, these cases show that leadership at scale is not a singular trait. It is a disciplined response to recurring tensions. Alignment, durability, adaptation, orchestration, and balance emerge as distinct leadership moves exercised under different configurations of constraint. The chapters that follow explore these moves not as abstract principles, but as decisions made in real systems characterized by imperfect authority, uneven capacity, and contested legitimacy.

DOI: 10.4324/9781003685821-6

4 Aligning Without Control

Eradicating Smallpox

The Scale Challenge

I returned to the case of smallpox during a public talk not because it was dramatic or timely, but because it unsettled me. Smallpox remains one of the few cases in global health where a proven intervention did not stall at pilot scale, donor fatigue, or shifting political priorities, but was sustained long enough and coordinated broadly enough to achieve global impact. I revisited it not as a celebratory story, but because it conflicted with what I was seeing elsewhere in global health, where strong evidence so often failed to translate into lasting change.[1]

During that talk, I asked audiences to imagine a counterfactual world in which the smallpox vaccine had never been scaled. The vaccine itself had existed for more than two centuries. What changed history was not discovery, but the willingness and capacity to coordinate action across countries, systems, and communities over time. Smallpox forces a leadership question: how do you align actors you cannot command—long enough, and well enough, to change history?

That question is often obscured in how the smallpox story is told.

The eradication of smallpox is frequently described as a triumph of vaccination technology. Yet vaccination alone does not explain its success. By the late 1960s, an effective smallpox vaccine had existed for decades.[2] What remained unresolved was a scale problem: how to coordinate action globally across sovereign states, weak health systems, and deeply heterogeneous social and political contexts.[3,4]

The central challenge of smallpox eradication was therefore global coordination without global authority. No institution possessed the power to compel national governments to comply with eradication strategies, direct subnational implementation, or ensure community participation. The effort unfolded amid Cold War geopolitics, postcolonial state formation, fragile administrative systems, and widespread mistrust of public authority in many endemic regions.[5,6]

Scale was unforgiving. Eradication required eliminating transmission everywhere, including in settings where routine health services were minimal, geographic access was limited, and communities sometimes concealed cases to avoid stigma or coercive interventions. A single missed outbreak could undermine progress across entire regions.[3] The problem leaders faced was not simply how to expand delivery, but how to sustain coordinated action across jurisdictions

DOI: 10.4324/9781003685821-7

and social boundaries where no actor could enforce compliance. Scaling up the smallpox vaccine was not a single act, but a sustained process requiring mass production of stable, freeze-dried vaccines, rapid global distribution, continuous surveillance, and coordinated field operations over many years, culminating in eradication in 1980.[3,7]

Framed in this way, smallpox eradication is not primarily a story of program delivery. It is a case of leadership at scale, centered on the challenge of mobilizing collective action across fragmented systems when authority, capacity, and trust are unevenly distributed. What makes smallpox compelling to me is not that it worked, but that it worked under conditions that most contemporary scale efforts still struggle to navigate.

Leadership Problem Definition

The leadership challenges of smallpox eradication were fundamentally non-technical. While scientific expertise was essential, it did not resolve the core problems leaders confronted. What the smallpox case makes clear is that scientific breakthroughs alone were insufficient; eradication depended on leadership capable of coordinating action across fragmented systems and sustained political commitment.[4,8] What mattered was how leaders translated evidence into coordinated action across systems that were fragmented, contested, and often fragile.

First, authority was fragmented. The global eradication effort operated through the World Health Organization, which held convening power and technical legitimacy but lacked enforcement authority. National governments retained sovereignty over health policy, financing, and personnel, while subnational officials often controlled access to communities and frontline resources. Leadership therefore depended on persuasion, negotiation, and alignment rather than command.[5,9]

Second, political resistance was persistent. Governments varied in their commitment to eradication, often balancing it against other pressing health and development priorities. In some contexts, external involvement in domestic health programs was viewed with suspicion, particularly during the Cold War. Leaders could not assume stable political support or uniform buy-in for a globally defined objective.[6]

Third, health systems were weak and uneven. Many endemic countries lacked reliable routine immunization platforms, functioning surveillance systems, and sufficient health workforce capacity. Transport networks were limited, cold chains fragile, and administrative reach inconsistent. Leaders could not rely on existing delivery systems to achieve scale; instead, they had to design strategies that worked around these structural constraints while still depending on the same systems for implementation.[3,4]

Fourth, trust and compliance were uncertain. In several settings, smallpox control measures were associated with coercion, quarantine, or intrusive surveillance. Families sometimes concealed cases to avoid stigma or disruption, undermining detection and response. Technical authority did not translate automatically into social legitimacy, making community engagement a central leadership challenge rather than a peripheral concern.[10,11]

Finally, information was incomplete and unreliable. Surveillance data were often delayed, inaccurate, or politically filtered. Leaders were required to make high-stakes decisions about strategy and resource allocation under conditions of persistent uncertainty.[12]

Taken together, these conditions defined a leadership problem centered on alignment under constraint. The challenge was not to optimize a technical intervention, but to mobilize collective action across political, institutional, and social boundaries in the absence of control. This distinction marks the boundary between leadership and management in large-scale health initiatives. When I read the smallpox history, what stands out is how little of the progress depended on formal authority. Leadership emerged instead from the ability to align actors who could not be commanded and to govern systems that were fragile, incomplete, and politically constrained.

What Scaled and What Nearly Failed

The smallpox eradication effort scaled successfully, but not smoothly. Its trajectory was punctuated by moments where progress stalled or nearly reversed, making leadership most visible at the edge of failure. These near-failures reveal how much progress depended on leaders who could adapt strategy in real time, sustain morale during prolonged uncertainty, and navigate ethical dilemmas in conflict-affected settings without losing legitimacy.

Surveillance failures were among the most serious threats to scale. Field experience in West and Central Africa demonstrated how rapid surveillance-response loops could overcome weak routine systems when local authority and trust were secured.[13] In several contexts, particularly in South Asia, cases were deliberately concealed by families and local officials seeking to avoid quarantine, stigma, or administrative scrutiny. These breakdowns undermined containment efforts and exposed the fragility of surveillance systems that depended on voluntary reporting.[3,10,12]

Logistical bottlenecks also repeatedly threatened progress. Transport limitations, fuel shortages, and workforce constraints delayed outbreak response in remote or insecure areas. In some regions, the inability to move teams or supplies quickly allowed transmission chains to persist longer than anticipated.[4]

Political pushback posed another recurring risk. Changes in government leadership, shifting national priorities, or resistance from subnational authorities periodically disrupted implementation. The eradication effort relied on sustained political goodwill that could not be taken for granted and had to be continually renewed.[6]

What I take from these near-failures is that scale is not sustained by perfection, but by leadership capacity to absorb shocks without losing legitimacy. Financing uncertainty further exposed vulnerabilities. Although eradication was relatively inexpensive compared to other global health initiatives, funding was neither automatic nor guaranteed. Interruptions in financial support created operational cliffs that leaders had to manage through reallocation, prioritization, and advocacy.[3]

What ultimately scaled was not a flawless system, but a capacity to recover from breakdowns. Leadership mattered most when failures were acknowledged quickly, strategies were adjusted, and legitimacy was rebuilt before setbacks cascaded.

What smallpox leaves unresolved is not whether leadership mattered, but how it was exercised across levels. Local leaders often determined access, trust, and speed, while global leadership shaped coherence and persistence. Much of what enabled progress in conflict-affected settings remains poorly documented, particularly the informal negotiations, ethical compromises, and personal toll borne by those involved. These gaps do not weaken the case. They underscore how much leadership at scale operates beyond formal authority and recorded protocol.

Leadership Decisions Under Constraint

The success of smallpox eradication rested on a series of leadership moves that explicitly acknowledged these constraints and worked through them rather than attempting to eliminate them.

One of the most consequential decisions was to prioritize interrupting transmission over maximizing coverage. Early eradication strategies emphasized mass vaccination targets that were poorly aligned with system capacity. Leaders gradually shifted toward a surveillance-and-containment approach, redefining success around the rapid identification and isolation of outbreaks rather than blanket coverage.[3,4] This reframing represented a leadership judgment about what form of scale was achievable under real-world conditions. This shift is often described as technical adaptation, but I read it as a leadership decision to abandon comforting metrics in favor of strategies that could survive real system limits.

First, leaders chose deliberate simplification. Surveillance systems were redesigned to emphasize timely, actionable information rather than comprehensive reporting. Vaccination strategies were narrowed to ring containment around confirmed cases, reducing logistical complexity and allowing scarce resources to be concentrated where they would have the greatest impact.[9] These choices reflected an understanding that complexity itself was a threat to scale.

Second, leaders intentionally decentralized operational authority. While overall strategy and goals were coordinated centrally, frontline teams were granted discretion to adapt tactics to local contexts, negotiate access with community leaders, and respond rapidly to emerging challenges. Success depended less on strict protocol adherence than on responsiveness, improvisation, and local problem-solving.[4]

Finally, leaders made careful distinctions between what should remain exceptional and what should be absorbed into existing systems. Emergency funding streams, rapid-response teams, and extraordinary authority were kept time-bound and purpose-specific to avoid overwhelming fragile health systems. In contrast, surveillance practices and reporting norms were gradually integrated into national health structures, enhancing durability without requiring wholesale system transformation.[3]

Together, these leadership moves illustrate that smallpox eradication advanced not through technical optimization alone, but through strategic decisions about focus, simplicity, authority, and adaptation under constraint. Table 4.1 summarizes the major constraints leaders faced and the strategic decisions that enabled eradication to proceed despite them.

Table 4.1 Leadership Decisions Under Constraint in Smallpox Eradication

Constraint	*Technically Plausible Response*	*Leadership Decision*	*Contribution to Scale*
1. Fragmented authority across sovereign states	Centralized command-and-control through international agencies	Leaders relied on persuasion, negotiation, and voluntary alignment rather than enforcement	Enabled cooperation without undermining national sovereignty, sustaining participation in the absence of global authority
2. Weak and uneven health systems	Uniform mass vaccination targets applied across settings	Strategy shifted toward surveillance and containment calibrated to local system capacity	Allowed eradication to proceed even where routine delivery systems were minimal or unreliable
3. Logistical complexity and scarce resources	Comprehensive reporting requirements and standardized procedures	Surveillance and response protocols were deliberately simplified	Reduced operational burden, limited failure points, and supported rapid field-level action
4. Social resistance and low trust	Coercive enforcement of vaccination and case reporting	Operational authority was decentralized, allowing local adaptation and negotiation	Preserved legitimacy and compliance by enabling context-sensitive engagement with communities
5. Persistent uncertainty and incomplete information	Delayed action pending comprehensive or verified data	Leaders acted under uncertainty, adjusting strategy iteratively as information improved	Prevented paralysis and supported timely containment despite imperfect surveillance
6. Risk of overwhelming fragile health systems	Permanent parallel delivery and governance structures	Emergency measures were kept time-bound, with selective integration into national systems	Achieved rapid impact while limiting long-term distortion of existing institutions

Tensions and Trade-Offs

Leadership during the smallpox eradication campaign was defined by persistent tensions rather than clear-cut choices. These tensions did not resolve over time; instead, they had to be continuously managed as scale expanded.

One central tension was global coordination versus national sovereignty. Effective eradication required alignment across borders, shared surveillance standards, and coordinated response strategies. Yet national governments retained full authority over health policy and implementation. International leaders could not impose uniform approaches without risking political resistance or withdrawal of cooperation. This coordination problem has been characterized as a global collective action dilemma, in which eradication succeeded only because incentives, costs, and reputational pressures were aligned across states despite the absence of enforcement authority.[14] Progress depended on navigating this tension through diplomacy, accommodation, and selective flexibility rather than enforcement.[4,6] Progress also depended on diplomatic leadership that sustained cooperation across ideological divides during the Cold War. Vaccine supply from the Soviet Union, operational expertise from the United States, and contributions from multiple countries were held together through negotiation rather than authority.

Of these tensions, speed versus legitimacy proved the most persistent. Rapid detection and containment were essential to interrupt transmission, particularly in high-density or mobile populations. However, accelerated response efforts often clashed with local norms, consent processes, and community trust. Aggressive containment could provoke resistance, case concealment, or disengagement. Leaders were forced to balance urgency with social legitimacy, adjusting tactics to preserve cooperation even when speed was compromised.[9,10]

A third tension emerged between standardization and contextual adaptation. Global eradication required some degree of consistency in surveillance definitions, reporting protocols, and response thresholds. At the same time, rigid standardization proved unworkable across highly diverse settings. Leaders had to tolerate variation in how strategies were implemented locally while maintaining coherence around overarching goals.[3]

Finally, leaders faced the tension between emergency authority and long-term institutions. Exceptional powers, funding mechanisms, and operational arrangements enabled rapid action but risked bypassing or undermining fragile health systems. Leaders had to decide when to act outside existing structures and when to embed practices within them, knowing that either choice carried long-term consequences.[4]

These tensions underscore that leadership at scale does not eliminate trade-offs. It consists of repeatedly making imperfect decisions under conditions where all available options carry risk.

This is why I am wary when smallpox is invoked as a simple model for scale. Its success rested not on resolving these tensions, but on leaders repeatedly managing them without expecting clean solutions.

Leadership Moves

Leadership in the eradication of smallpox was not expressed through authority or technical mastery. It emerged through disciplined judgments that enabled alignment across fragmented systems where compliance could not be compelled.

- **Define the scale problem before designing the solution.** Leaders reframed eradication from a vaccination coverage challenge to a coordination problem across sovereign actors. This shift redirected attention from volume metrics to the conditions required for sustained collective action.
- **Redefine success in ways that align with system capacity.** Rather than equating scale with universal coverage, leaders prioritized surveillance and containment calibrated to what fragile systems could execute reliably. This aligned ambition with operational reality.
- **Simplify to protect execution under strain.** Surveillance systems and response protocols were narrowed to what was actionable in real time. Simplification reduced failure points and enabled rapid field-level adaptation without overwhelming weak administrative structures.
- **Centralize purpose while decentralizing operational authority.** Shared standards and global direction provided coherence, while frontline teams retained discretion to negotiate access and adapt tactics locally. This balance preserved legitimacy and responsiveness without fragmenting strategy.
- **Act under uncertainty and recalibrate openly.** Leaders did not wait for perfect information. They treated surveillance gaps, resistance, and setbacks as signals for adjustment rather than grounds for paralysis.
- **Distinguish emergency instruments from institutional foundations.** Exceptional measures enabled speed, but leaders selectively integrated surveillance practices into national systems while keeping extraordinary authority time-bound.

References

1. Ezezika O. TEDxMcMasterU; Hamilton (ON). Scaling breakthroughs to save lives [Internet]. 2025. Available from: https://www.youtube.com/watch?v=Qn8yM2gX-Z8
2. Fenner F. Global eradication of smallpox [with discussion]. Rev Infect Dis. 1982; 4(5):916–30.
3. Fenner F, Henderson DA, Arita I, Jezek Z, Ladnyi ID. Smallpox and its eradication. Geneva, Switzerland: World Health Organization; 1988.
4. Henderson DA. Smallpox: the death of a disease: the inside story of eradicating a worldwide killer. Amherst, NY: Prometheus Books; 2009.
5. Henderson DA, Klepac P. Lessons from the eradication of smallpox: an interview with D. A. Henderson. Philos Trans R Soc B Biol Sci. 2013 Aug 5;368(1623):20130113. doi:10.1098/rstb.2013.0113 PubMed PMID: 23798700; PubMed Central PMCID: PMC3720050.
6. Manela E. The right to health: global health and the Cold War. Cambridge, MA: Harvard University Press; 2010.

7. Fenner F, World Health Organization. The eradication of smallpox. Geneva: World Health Organization; 1976. Report No.: WHO/SE/76.83.
8. Henderson DA. Eradication: lessons from the past. Bull World Health Organ. 1998;76 Suppl 2(Suppl 2):17–21. PubMed PMID: 10063668; PubMed Central PMCID: PMC2305698.
9. Brilliant LB. The management of smallpox eradication in India [Internet]. Ann Arbor: University of Michigan Press; 1985. Available from: https://www.zero-pox.info/other_docs/brilliant_mgmt_spox_india.pdf
10. Greenough P. Intimidation, coercion and resistance in the final stages of the South Asian Smallpox Eradication Campaign, 1973–1975. Soc Sci Med. 1995 Sep;41(5):633–45. doi:10.1016/0277–9536(95)00035-6 PubMed PMID: 7502097.
11. Juran L, Trivedi J, Kolivras KN. Considering the "public" in public health: popular resistance to the Smallpox Eradication Programme in India. Indian J Med Ethics. 2017 Apr-Jun;2(2):104–111. doi:10.20529/IJME.2017.025. PMID: 28512076.
12. Henderson DA. Surveillance of smallpox. Int J Epidemiol. 1976 Mar;5(1):19–28. doi:10.1093/ije/5.1.19 PubMed PMID: 1262108.
13. Foege WH, Millar JD, Henderson DA. Smallpox eradication in West and Central Africa. Bull World Health Organ. 1975;52(2):209–22. PubMed PMID: 1083309; PubMed Central PMCID: PMC2366358.
14. Barrett S. The smallpox eradication game. Public Choice. 2007;130(1/2):179–207.

5 Sustaining Scale Under Implementation Strain

Malaria Bed Nets

The Scale Challenge

The scale challenge in malaria bed net delivery was never about scientific uncertainty. Insecticide-treated nets were shown early on to reduce malaria morbidity and mortality across multiple epidemiological settings.[1,2] Their effectiveness was sufficiently established that debate shifted quickly from whether nets worked to how they could be delivered widely enough, consistently enough, and long enough to matter.[3,4]

What leaders encountered instead was a problem of durability under strain. Mass distribution campaigns produced dramatic gains in ownership, yet those gains repeatedly eroded. Nets tore, insecticide efficacy declined, households repurposed or abandoned them, and replacement systems failed to keep pace. Across Tanzania, Nigeria, Kenya, Ghana, Zambia, and Cambodia, the same pattern emerged: impressive short-term coverage followed by gradual attrition.[3,5–9]

Scaling malaria bed nets therefore exposed a central paradox of global health scale. The intervention was simple, but the system required to sustain it was not. Leaders were asked to hold together financing cycles, procurement pipelines, transport systems, community behavior, and political commitment over time horizons that far exceeded donor attention spans.

This challenge was compounded by geography and poverty. Many of the highest-burden regions were also those with weak infrastructure, limited retail markets, and overstretched health systems. Distance to distribution points, seasonal migration, housing design, heat, and sleeping arrangements all shaped whether nets were used even when they were present.[8]

The leadership problem was therefore not how to expand access once, but how to prevent collapse after scale. That distinction matters. Scale here was not a moment of achievement but a condition that had to be continuously defended. These failures were not accidental. They reflected structural limits on what leaders could control once interventions entered everyday life.

Leadership Problem Definition

The leadership challenges associated with scaling malaria bed nets were fundamentally non-technical and globally shared. By the time insecticide-treated nets

DOI: 10.4324/9781003685821-8

became a central pillar of malaria control policy, their biological effectiveness was well established across diverse epidemiological settings.[2,10] What remained unresolved was not whether bed nets worked, but whether leaders could sustain protection at population scale when effectiveness depended on behaviors, maintenance, and replacement processes that lay beyond their direct control.

Across Africa, Southeast Asia, and Latin America, leaders confronted a common structural condition best described as authority without command. Bed nets could be financed, procured, and distributed through centralized systems, but their impact depended on household-level decisions made in private spaces. Leaders could mandate procurement volumes, campaign schedules, and coverage targets, yet they could not enforce nightly use, correct installation, repair, or timely replacement. Once a net entered a household, formal authority largely ended. This created a condition of scale without enforcement, in which leaders were held accountable for outcomes they could not directly govern.[8]

Compounding this constraint was fragmented accountability across the delivery system. Financing flowed primarily from international donors, procurement was often centralized at national level, and distribution relied on a heterogeneous mix of public agencies, non-governmental organizations (NGOs), faith-based groups, and private retailers. Use and care, however, remained the responsibility of households. No single actor owned long-term protection outcomes when nets deteriorated, use declined, or replacement cycles failed. This fragmentation has been documented not only in African programs, but also in Southeast Asia and Latin America, where overlapping mandates and misaligned incentives complicated adaptation and slowed corrective action.[8]

Within this institutional landscape, leaders everywhere faced a persistent equity–sustainability dilemma. Free mass distribution campaigns powerfully advanced equity by reaching populations least able to access markets, including rural, poor, and marginalized households. Yet repeated reliance on free delivery weakened private supply chains and made replacement dependent on donor cycles rather than net durability or household demand. Market-based and social marketing approaches improved continuity and normalized replacement, but systematically excluded poor, rural, or Indigenous populations unless heavily subsidized. This dilemma was not geographically bounded. It reappeared wherever leaders attempted to scale household-based interventions under conditions of inequality.

Leaders also confronted a profound visibility gap between coverage and protection. Ownership could be measured, reported, and celebrated. Use, durability, and consistent protection were harder to observe and rarely rewarded. Across regions, this skewed decision-making toward strategies that maximized short-term coverage rather than long-term stewardship, reinforcing success at the moment of delivery while allowing erosion over time.[8]

A further constraint emerged from a temporal mismatch between intervention needs and governance cycles. Bed nets require sustained attention over multiple years, including replacement, financing continuity, and periodic re-engagement with households. Leadership incentives, however, were often aligned with shorter donor funding windows, campaign timelines, and political calendars. Early success generated momentum, but protection eroded most often in the long tail of scale, when visibility declined and adaptation slowed.

These dynamics are illustrated vividly in the Mekong region of Southeast Asia. As malaria transmission declined in parts of Cambodia, Laos, and Vietnam, leaders observed a paradoxical pattern: net ownership remained high, yet consistent use declined. Households perceived malaria as a diminishing threat, while discomfort in hot, humid conditions reduced nightly adherence. At the same time, insecticide resistance weakened the effectiveness of standard nets, further complicating the relationship between access and protection.[8] Leaders responded not by doubling down on distribution, but by recalibrating strategy. Messaging shifted from universal risk to targeted communication focused on forest workers and border populations, and delivery models narrowed from mass campaigns to more selective approaches. These adaptations improved sustainability among high-risk groups but reduced overall coverage, reproducing the same equity–sustainability tension observed in African and Latin American settings.

Taken together, these conditions define a single global leadership problem: governing durability without direct control. The challenge was not to optimize a technology or perfect delivery, but to sustain protection across fragmented systems in which authority, accountability, trust, and time horizons rarely aligned. Leadership at scale was exercised not through command, but through judgment about how to manage inevitable trade-offs over time.

What Scaled and What Nearly Failed

What ultimately scaled in malaria bed net delivery was not a stable or self-sustaining system, but a capacity for repair under recurring strain. Coverage expanded, eroded, and was rebuilt repeatedly. Progress was uneven, reversible, and contingent on leadership responses to failure rather than on initial design quality.

Near-failures were not episodic; they were structural. In Tanzania and Nigeria, national campaigns achieved rapid increases in household ownership, yet protection declined sharply as nets aged and replacement systems lagged behind need. The gap between distribution cycles and net durability created periods where nominal coverage masked declining effectiveness.[5,8] In these contexts, scale nearly failed not because delivery was impossible, but because continuity was underprioritized.

In Southeast Asia, particularly Cambodia and Laos, the problem took a different form. Distribution systems functioned, but biological and behavioral shifts undermined impact. Insecticide resistance reduced net effectiveness, while changes in vector biting patterns and sleeping practices limited protection. Leadership failures here were not logistical, but adaptive. Where leaders were slow to revise assumptions about vector behavior or to introduce complementary strategies, scale lost relevance even as coverage persisted.[10,11]

Kenya and parts of Uganda exposed another vulnerability: logistics and last-mile delivery. Transport bottlenecks, storage constraints, and seasonal inaccessibility delayed net delivery to remote communities. In these cases, scale nearly failed at the margins, where weak infrastructure magnified small disruptions into prolonged protection gaps.[8]

What preserved scale was not adherence to original plans, but leadership willingness to intervene mid-course. Leaders redesigned nets to improve durability and usability, adjusted financing mechanisms to shorten replacement cycles, expanded delivery channels beyond campaigns, and revised messaging to align with lived realities. Where leaders treated breakdowns as signals requiring adaptation, systems recovered. Where they defended single models or relied on outdated assumptions, progress stalled or reversed.

The lesson is not that malaria bed nets succeeded universally. It is that scale endured where leadership capacity absorbed shocks rather than denying them, and where failure triggered recalibration rather than retrenchment.

Leadership Decisions Under Constraint

Leadership responses to these constraints were expressed through a series of consequential judgments rather than through technical innovation alone.

A critical decision involved redefining what scale meant. Instead of treating coverage targets as endpoints, leaders reframed scale as a dynamic condition requiring continuous replenishment, shifting attention toward replacement cycles, durability, and sustained use.

Building on this reframing, leaders rejected single-model scale. Early debates framed delivery as a choice between free distribution and market-based approaches. Leaders in Tanzania, Kenya, and Ghana gradually abandoned this binary, opting instead for hybrid systems that combined free provision for vulnerable groups with subsidized or commercial channels for others.[5,12,13]

Tanzania's National Voucher Scheme illustrates this judgment. By subsidizing nets through retail outlets for pregnant women and infants, leaders preserved market participation while expanding access. This approach was more complex to manage and less photogenic than mass campaigns, but it reflected a leadership decision to trade simplicity for resilience.

Leaders also made a deliberate choice to decentralize operational authority. Community health workers, local NGOs, and informal distributors were granted discretion to adapt messaging, timing, and follow-up. In rural Kenya and Tanzania, community-based distribution increased reach in areas where formal health facilities were inaccessible.[8] This decentralization came at the cost of uniformity but improved legitimacy and responsiveness.

Another judgment involved embracing adaptation over standardization. Human-centered design research conducted in Ghana and Nigeria revealed that discomfort, heat retention, and aesthetic preferences shaped net use more strongly than health messaging alone.[14–16] Leaders responded by supporting redesigned nets and context-specific education strategies, accepting that a single "optimal" product was incompatible with diverse living conditions.[5,8,17]

Finally, leaders made a critical interpretive decision: they treated resistance and non-use as diagnostic signals rather than compliance failures. Misuse prompted redesign, not punishment. Declining use triggered investigation rather than blame. This stance allowed systems to learn rather than fracture.

Tensions and Trade-Offs

Leadership in malaria bed net scale-up was defined not by problems that could be solved once and for all, but by tensions that had to be navigated repeatedly over time. These were not dilemmas with optimal solutions. They were enduring trade-offs that resurfaced at every phase of scale, demanding judgment rather than resolution.

The most persistent tension was between equity and sustainability. Free distribution campaigns dramatically improved fairness and achieved rapid gains in coverage, particularly among the poorest and most remote populations. Yet over time, reliance on free delivery weakened local markets and made replacement dependent on donor cycles rather than on wear, demand, or household priorities. Market-based approaches offered greater continuity and normalized replacement, but systematically excluded those least able to pay. Hybrid models that combined targeted subsidies, campaign distribution, and retail markets reduced these extremes but never eliminated them, requiring leaders to continuously recalibrate as economic conditions, donor priorities, and population needs shifted.

A second tension lay between speed and legitimacy. Mass campaigns excelled at moving quickly, delivering millions of nets in compressed timeframes during outbreaks or funding windows. But speed often came at the cost of community engagement. Nets were delivered faster than trust could be built, and faster than norms around use could form, leading to misuse, neglect, or selective adoption. Slower, participatory approaches fostered legitimacy and alignment with lived realities, but delayed protection and increased costs. Leaders were repeatedly forced to decide when urgency justified bypassing deliberation, and when legitimacy was worth the wait.

A third tension emerged between global coherence and local adaptation. Standardized targets, indicators, and reporting frameworks made scale legible to donors and facilitated coordination across countries. Yet uniform designs faltered in the face of diverse housing structures, climates, and sleeping arrangements. What worked in one setting failed in another. Leaders had to tolerate variation and improvisation while maintaining enough coherence to preserve credibility, comparability, and funding flows.

Finally, leaders navigated a persistent tension between donor accountability and local reality. Reporting systems rewarded what could be easily counted: nets delivered, households reached, campaigns completed. Far less visible were patterns of use, durability, and protection over time. Leaders had to decide whether to optimize for metrics that secured future funding or for practices that sustained protection, knowing that these goals often diverged.

Taken together, these tensions were not signs of weak leadership or flawed design. They were the terrain on which leadership operated. Effective leadership did not eliminate trade-offs; it managed them—again and again—under conditions of uncertainty, inequality, and constraint.

Leadership Moves

Leadership in malaria bed net scale-up was not expressed through authority, technical mastery, or fidelity to a preferred delivery model. It was expressed through judgment exercised under persistent constraint.

- **Redefine scale as continuity rather than coverage.** Rather than treating distribution targets as endpoints, leaders framed success around sustained protection over time. This redirected attention toward replacement cycles, durability, and consistent use, even when these dimensions were harder to measure and less visible to funders.
- **Reject purity in favor of hybrid delivery systems.** Rather than committing exclusively to free distribution or market-based channels, leaders combined mass campaigns, vouchers, subsidies, and retail markets. This pluralism reflected the judgment that resilience required multiple pathways, even at the cost of administrative complexity.
- **Decentralize legitimacy while centralizing intent.** Strategic direction and financing remained centralized, but trust was cultivated locally. Community leaders, health workers, shopkeepers, and informal intermediaries became essential actors in sustaining use, particularly where state authority alone could not secure compliance.
- **Treat resistance and non-use as signals of misalignment.** Patterns of misuse, abandonment, or skepticism were interpreted as evidence that intervention design and social context were not yet aligned. Leaders responded through redesign, retiming, and revised communication rather than coercive enforcement.
- **Build replacement into the scaling model.** Durable protection depends on what happens after the campaign ends. Leaders should plan financing, procurement, household re-engagement, and monitoring around net deterioration and replacement needs rather than treating distribution as the endpoint.
- **Accept trade-offs without expecting resolution.** Equity was weighed against sustainability, speed against legitimacy, and standardization against adaptation. Leadership did not eliminate these tensions but managed them long enough for impact to accumulate.

References

1. Gamble C, Ekwaru JP, ter Kuile FO. Insecticide-treated nets for preventing malaria in pregnancy. Cochrane Database Syst Rev. 2006 Apr 19;2006(2):CD003755. doi: 10.1002/14651858.CD003755.pub2 PubMed PMID: 16625591; PubMed Central PMCID: PMC6532581.
2. Lengeler C. Insecticide-treated bed nets and curtains for preventing malaria. Cochrane Database Syst Rev. 2004;(2):CD000363. doi:10.1002/14651858.CD000363.pub2 PubMed PMID: 15106149.
3. Bhatt S, Weiss DJ, Cameron E, Bisanzio D, Mappin B, Dalrymple U, et al. The effect of malaria control on Plasmodium falciparum in Africa between 2000 and 2015. Nature. 2015 Oct 8;526(7572):207–11. doi:10.1038/nature15535 PubMed PMID: 26375008; PubMed Central PMCID: PMC4820050.
4. Jamison DT, Breman JG, Measham AR, Alleyne G, Claeson M, Evans DB, et al., editors. Disease Control Priorities in Developing Countries [Internet]. 2nd ed. Washington (DC):

The International Bank for Reconstruction and Development / The World Bank; 2006 [cited 2026 Feb 4]. Available from: http://www.ncbi.nlm.nih.gov/books/NBK11728/ PubMed PMID: 21250309.

5. Ezezika O. Scaling up health innovations in Africa. Toronto: University of Toronto Press; 2025.
6. Ezezika O, El-Bakri Y, Nadarajah A, Barrett K. Implementation of insecticide-treated malaria bed nets in Tanzania: a systematic review. J Glob Health Rep. 2022 Aug 15;6. doi:10.29392/001c.37363
7. Kilian A, Byamukama W, Pigeon O, Gimnig J, Atieli F, Koekemoer L, et al. Evidence for a useful life of more than three years for a polyester-based long-lasting insecticidal mosquito net in Western Uganda. Malar J. 2011 Oct 13;10:299. doi:10.1186/1475–2875-10–299 PubMed PMID: 21992483; PubMed Central PMCID: PMC3212829.
8. Pulford J, Hetzel MW, Bryant M, Siba PM, Mueller I. Reported reasons for not using a mosquito net when one is available: a review of the published literature. Malar J. 2011 Apr 11;10(1):83. doi:10.1186/1475–2875-10–83
9. World Health Organization. Guidelines for monitoring the durability of long-lasting insecticidal mosquito nets under operational conditions. Geneva: WHO Press, 2011. Report No.: WHO/HTM/NTD/WHOPES/2011.5
10. Pryce J, Richardson M, Lengeler C. Insecticide-treated nets for preventing malaria. Cochrane Database Syst Rev. 2018 Nov 6;11(11):CD000363. doi:10.1002/14651858.CD000363.pub3 PubMed PMID: 30398672; PubMed Central PMCID: PMC6418392.
11. World Health Organization. World malaria report 2020 [Internet]. World Health Organization; 2020. Available from: https://www.who.int/publications/i/item/9789240015791
12. Hanson K, Marchant T, Nathan R, Mponda H, Jones C, Bruce J, et al. Household ownership and use of insecticide treated nets among target groups after implementation of a national voucher programme in the United Republic of Tanzania: plausibility study using three annual cross sectional household surveys. BMJ. 2009 Jul 2;339:b2434. doi:10.1136/bmj.b2434 PubMed PMID: 19574316; PubMed Central PMCID: PMC2714691.
13. Mulligan JA, Yukich J, Hanson K. Costs and effects of the Tanzanian national voucher scheme for insecticide-treated nets. Malar J. 2008 Feb 15;7:32. doi:10.1186/1475–2875–7–32 PubMed PMID: 18279509; PubMed Central PMCID: PMC2279140.
14. Aikins MK, Pickering H, Greenwood BM. Attitudes to malaria, traditional practices and bednets (mosquito nets) as vector control measures: a comparative study in five west African countries. J Trop Med Hyg. 1994 Apr;97(2):81–6. PubMed PMID: 8170007.
15. Bonsra EA, Osei PA, Sekyi AG, Kyere GA. Insecticide-treated bed nets (ITN) ownership and utilization patterns among caregivers with children under five years: a community-based cross-sectional study in Battor, North Tongu District, Ghana. PLOS Glob Public Health. 2025 Feb 6;5(2):e0004228. doi:10.1371/journal.pgph.0004228
16. Iloh GUP, Amadi AN, Obiukwu CE, Njoku PU, Ofoedu JN, Okafor GOC. Family biosocial variables influencing the use of insecticide treated nets for children in Eastern Nigeria. J Fam Community Med. 2013;20(1):12–9. doi:10.4103/2230–8229.108178 PubMed PMID: 23723726; PubMed Central PMCID: PMC3663159.
17. Winch PJ, Makemba AM, Kamazima SR, Lurie M, Lwihula GK, Premji Z, et al. Local terminology for febrile illnesses in Bagamoyo District, Tanzania and its impact on the design of a community-based malaria control programme. Soc Sci Med. 1996 Apr;42(7):1057–67. doi:10.1016/0277–9536(95)00293-6 PubMed PMID: 8730911.

6 Adapting Under Constraint

Epidemic Meningitis Elimination

The Scale Challenge

Scaling health innovations in low-resource settings is often framed as a logistical problem: weak infrastructure, unreliable supply chains, shortages of personnel, and limited financing. These constraints matter, but their persistence suggests a deeper issue. The core challenge is leadership under conditions of scale: making consequential judgments when systems are fragile, authority is dispersed, and orthodox delivery models do not fit reality.

This chapter examines MenAfriVac through the Meningitis Vaccine Project as a case of adaptation as strategy. The achievement was not simply developing a vaccine. It was redesigning both the intervention and its delivery so prevention could function within real system limits without lowering safety expectations or eroding trust.

Meningococcal meningitis has long posed a severe public health threat in sub-Saharan Africa. Countries within the African Meningitis Belt, stretching from Senegal to Ethiopia, experienced recurrent, cyclical epidemics with devastating consequences. The largest recorded epidemic, in 1996–1997, resulted in more than 250,000 cases and approximately 50,000 deaths across the region.[1,2]

Despite decades of scientific progress and the availability of polysaccharide meningococcal vaccines, preventive delivery at scale remained elusive well into the early 2000s. Health systems responded reactively, mobilizing emergency vaccination campaigns only after epidemics were already underway. These responses were logistically complex, politically charged, and often too late to prevent widespread transmission. The result was a recurring cycle of crisis response followed by periods of neglect once outbreaks subsided.[3]

The scale challenge confronting leaders was therefore not simply how to distribute a vaccine, but how to design an intervention and a delivery strategy capable of functioning within fragile health systems amid uncertainty, limited capacity, and uneven trust. Scale advanced because leaders deliberately redesigned both the product and its governance to function within constraint rather than waiting for systems to mature.

Defining the Leadership Problem

The core leadership problem at the heart of MenAfriVac's scale-up was not simply how to deliver a new vaccine, but how to redefine what "acceptable" vaccine

DOI: 10.4324/9781003685821-9

delivery looked like in health systems where standard global immunization assumptions did not hold. Prevailing norms of global vaccination practice, including continuous cold-chain integrity, predictable transport, stable staffing, and routine service platforms, were poorly aligned with the realities of the African Meningitis Belt, where meningitis risk was highest.

Across large swaths of the region, rural and peri-urban settings lacked reliable electricity, cold storage, and all-season road access. Health workers were overstretched, frequently responsible for multiple vertical programs, and operating with limited supervision and intermittent resupply. Seasonal migration patterns further complicated delivery and follow-up, particularly among pastoralist and mobile populations most vulnerable to epidemic meningitis.[4,5] Under these conditions, strict adherence to conventional vaccine handling protocols would have sharply constrained reach and delayed population-level protection.

This misalignment forced a leadership question that could not be resolved through technical optimization alone: Should health systems be expected to transform themselves to meet the intervention's requirements, or should the intervention be deliberately redesigned to fit system constraints as they existed? It implicated professional norms around vaccine safety, regulatory risk tolerance, and the credibility of global health institutions responsible for authorizing deviation from long-established standards.

Early deliberations about authorizing controlled temperature chain use made this leadership dilemma visible. Although emerging stability data suggested that MenAfriVac could tolerate limited exposure outside the traditional cold chain, authorizing controlled temperature chain use at scale required careful review and endorsement through WHO-linked technical and regulatory processes. The concern was not simply scientific uncertainty, but institutional precedent: authorizing deviation from orthodox cold-chain standards risked normalizing flexibility that regulators feared could be misapplied elsewhere. Marc LaForce, working through the Program for Appropriate Technology in Health (PATH) with the World Health Organization (WHO) and African ministries of health, pressed for a redefinition of acceptable practice under constraint. The judgment was to accept controlled, evidence-based operational risk in exchange for the more certain risk of limited reach if orthodoxy prevailed.

These challenges were compounded by historical mistrust linked to earlier outbreak responses, including the widely publicized 1996 Pfizer Trovan trial conducted during the meningitis outbreak in Kano, Nigeria, which reinforced suspicion toward externally driven interventions and toward departures from established standards during public health emergencies.[6] In this context, any relaxation of established vaccine-handling norms risked being interpreted not as adaptation, but as lowered standards for African populations.

The leadership problem, therefore, was one of authorization under constraint. Leaders had to determine whether, when, and how to sanction adaptive delivery strategies that expanded reach without eroding safety, legitimacy, or trust. Leadership was required not only to approve deviation from orthodoxy, but to sequence, frame, and govern that deviation in ways that frontline workers, national regulators, and communities could accept as both safe and justifiable.

Designing for System Constraints

Leadership in the MenAfriVac scale followed a consistent logic: simplify execution where system capacity was weakest and concentrate complexity where it could be managed. Delivery teams were asked to do fewer things well, while institutions absorbed evidence generation, regulatory justification, monitoring, and accountability.

Redesigning Delivery Assumptions to Fit System Realities

One of the most consequential leadership judgments during the MenAfriVac scale-up was the decision to permit vaccine delivery using a controlled temperature chain. Under this approach, MenAfriVac could be stored and transported outside the traditional cold chain for limited periods, within carefully defined and monitored temperature thresholds.[7] Strict adherence to this standard, however, had systematically constrained reach in areas at highest epidemiological risk.

Authorizing controlled temperature chain use required leaders to redefine what constituted acceptable risk. Evidence increasingly supported the stability, safety, and efficacy of MenAfriVac under controlled temperature conditions, but evidence alone rarely proved sufficient. Leaders had to legitimize deviation from entrenched practice, absorb institutional risk, and provide reassurance to frontline workers who would be held accountable for implementation outcomes.[7,8]

In Benin and other countries, controlled temperature chain use significantly expanded geographic coverage, reduced logistical complexity, and enabled vaccination teams to reach remote communities without dependence on ice packs or refrigeration.[7,8] It changed what vaccination teams could do in the last mile, especially in districts where power, refrigeration, and road access were least reliable.

Simplifying What Had to Move Through Weak Systems

A central leadership judgment during MenAfriVac's development was the decision to simplify relentlessly what frontline delivery systems would be required to handle, while accepting greater complexity elsewhere in the system. This orientation was advanced through the Meningitis Vaccine Project, a partnership between PATH and WHO, with Marc LaForce serving as Project Director at PATH and helping to sustain alignment among African ministries of health, WHO's technical bodies, and manufacturing partners.[9] Rather than optimizing for technical elegance or delivery platforms typical of high-income settings, leaders prioritized feasibility under severe and persistent system constraints.

MenAfriVac was deliberately developed as a single-dose vaccine, eliminating the need for follow-up doses and sharply reducing the administrative and logistical burden placed on overstretched health workers. Its ultra-low price point, approximately USD 0.50 per dose, was not simply a financing achievement but a leadership decision intended to enable rapid national adoption without long-term dependence on donor subsidies.[9,10] Product design was treated as a governance decision, not merely a technical feature.

Thermostability was treated as a strategic priority rather than a secondary technical feature. By enabling vaccine storage and transport under controlled temperature conditions, leaders reduced dependence on electricity, refrigeration, and ice packs, directly addressing one of the most persistent bottlenecks in rural vaccine delivery across the Meningitis Belt.

Crucially, simplification was selective. Leaders did not attempt to simplify governance, regulation, or surveillance. Instead, complexity and risk were intentionally absorbed at higher institutional levels. Global partners concentrated responsibility for evidence generation and regulatory justification, and they strengthened shared safety monitoring and accountability arrangements, allowing frontline systems to operate within manageable constraints.[8] This redistribution of complexity was itself a leadership act, because it shifted accountability for evidence, authorization, and monitoring upward, reducing the professional exposure of national managers and frontline workers implementing under uncertainty.

This figure shows how MenAfriVac scale-up depended on redistributing complexity and risk. Evidence generation, regulatory authorization, and safety monitoring were concentrated at institutional and global levels, while execution was simplified within frontline delivery systems. Scale was achieved through leadership decisions about where complexity and accountability should reside.

Figure 6.1 summarizes this redistribution of complexity and risk across levels of the system. Delivery was simplified at the point of execution, while evidence generation, regulatory authorization, surveillance, and accountability were concentrated in institutions better able to manage uncertainty. Leadership under scale was expressed through judgment about where complexity should reside, rather than attempts to eliminate it.

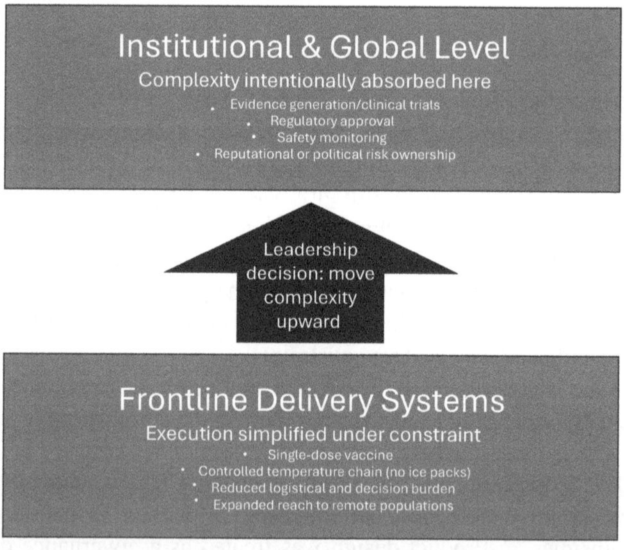

Figure 6.1 Shifting Complexity Up the System to Enable Scale

Centralizing Standards and Risk Ownership While Decentralizing Execution

A complementary leadership move involved separating authority over evidence from authority over action. Global institutions, including WHO and PATH, coordinated clinical trials, supported regulatory pathways, and strengthened post-introduction surveillance platforms, ensuring that decisions about safety and effectiveness were grounded in robust and centrally validated evidence.[10,11] This arrangement reflected a conscious effort by senior leaders to shield national program managers from bearing disproportionate political and professional risk when adopting unconventional delivery strategies such as controlled temperature chain use.

At the same time, operational authority was decentralized. National governments retained control over campaign timing, delivery modalities, workforce deployment, and integration into routine immunization schedules. This allowed adaptation to local epidemiological patterns, political conditions, and system capacity without fragmenting overall strategy. Leadership operated through buffering; global institutions absorbed uncertainty so national and local actors could execute decisively.

Mobilizing Commitment Without Formal Authority

The MenAfriVac initiative was also shaped by leadership exercised without formal hierarchical authority. Political commitment originated primarily within the region most affected. African leaders framed epidemic meningitis as an unacceptable and preventable burden and mobilized regional advocacy through mechanisms such as the Yaoundé Declaration.[8] This articulation of urgency generated what implementation science describes as "tension for change,"[12] creating political momentum that external partners could reinforce but not create themselves. Regional ownership made adaptation legitimate rather than externally imposed.

Leadership at the global level involved amplifying this regional demand, aligning donors, manufacturers, and technical agencies around a shared objective, and sustaining commitment beyond the initial visibility of mass campaigns.

Sustaining Momentum Through Adaptive Governance

Leadership did not end after the initial mass campaigns or after MenAfriVac began to be incorporated into national immunization strategies. Well before the COVID-19 pandemic, ongoing governance arrangements were required to manage transitions from mass campaigns to routine immunization and to respond to shifts in circulating meningococcal serogroups, including the emergence of non-A strains.[11] These challenges revealed that early success did not eliminate uncertainty, but instead changed the nature of the leadership task from rapid scale-up to long-term stewardship. Success shifted the leadership task from expansion to protection, with surveillance and adaptation becoming the core work.

Leaders emphasized surveillance, learning, and adaptation rather than treating post-introduction challenges as evidence of failure. The COVID-19 pandemic later exposed the fragility of these gains by disrupting routine immunization and surveillance systems, reinforcing rather than contradicting the earlier insight that sustaining scale depends on resilient governance rather than one-time technical success.[13]

Tensions and Trade-Offs

Leadership under conditions of scale required continuous navigation of tensions that could not be resolved once and for all, but instead had to be actively managed over time. These tensions were not incidental side effects of implementation. They were constitutive of the leadership challenge itself.

One of the most persistent tensions lay between safety assurance and delivery reach. Established immunization practice treated strict cold-chain compliance as a foundational safeguard, reinforcing professional norms around vaccine safety and accountability. In settings with reliable infrastructure, this standard functioned as intended. In the Meningitis Belt, however, it systematically constrained access to populations at highest epidemiological risk. Leaders faced a dilemma in which adherence to procedural safety norms reduced theoretical risk while allowing preventable epidemics to continue, whereas relaxing those norms expanded reach but required acceptance of calculated operational risk. This was not a choice between safety and recklessness, but between different distributions of risk. Leaders managed this tension by grounding deviation in evidence, defining explicit temperature thresholds, and pairing adaptation with monitoring and transparency. Rather than abandoning safety, they reinterpreted it at the population level, prioritizing protection against epidemic transmission over procedural purity.[7]

A second, equally consequential tension involved standardization versus contextual adaptation. Scale typically favors standardization. Uniform protocols simplify training, enable oversight, and facilitate coordination across countries and partners. Yet rigid standardization risked misalignment with the diverse social, infrastructural, and administrative realities across the Meningitis Belt. Their response was not to abandon standardization altogether, but to standardize at the level of principles rather than tactics. Safety monitoring, reporting requirements, and eligibility criteria were harmonized, while delivery modalities, campaign timing, and logistical arrangements were adapted locally. This distinction allowed coherence without rigidity, preserving legitimacy while enabling execution under constraint.[8,9]

Speed versus institutional caution constituted a third, recurring tension. Epidemics created intense pressure for rapid action, amplified by political scrutiny and donor expectations. At the same time, hasty decisions risked undermining trust, particularly in contexts shaped by historical grievances and skepticism toward external interventions. Leaders had to calibrate urgency carefully, especially when authorizing departures from established norms such as controlled temperature chain use. Acting too slowly would perpetuate preventable outbreaks; acting too quickly without sufficient deliberation could erode confidence among health workers and communities.

Across these tensions, leadership was less about choosing the "right" side than about sustaining balance under pressure. The capacity to hold competing imperatives in view, and to adjust as conditions changed, was central to making scale possible. These tensions frame MenAfriVac as a sequence of leadership judgments under constraint rather than a linear technical pathway.

What Scaled and What Nearly Failed

The epidemiological impact of MenAfriVac was both dramatic and unprecedented. Following widespread introduction, meningococcal serogroup A incidence declined by more than 99% in vaccinated populations, and large-scale epidemics attributable to that serogroup effectively disappeared across the Meningitis Belt.[10,14] For the first time in decades, countries that had endured recurring epidemic cycles experienced sustained interruption of transmission. This outcome validated the core leadership judgments that had shaped intervention design and delivery.

At the same time, the experience revealed the limits of scale and the fragility of success. Surveillance data from the post-introduction period documented outbreaks driven by non-A serogroups, reminding leaders that elimination of one pathogen variant did not equate to elimination of epidemic risk.[11] The monovalent nature of MenAfriVac, while instrumental in achieving rapid impact, also underscored the need for continued surveillance, adaptive vaccine strategies, and long-term investment in polyvalent solutions.

These vulnerabilities became more visible during the COVID-19 pandemic. Disruptions to routine immunization and mass campaigns led to millions of missed vaccinations across the region, raising concerns about resurgence and erosion of population immunity.[13] The pandemic exposed the extent to which scale depended not only on intervention design, but on sustained political attention, financing, and system functioning.

Leadership was most visible at these points of fragility. Rather than framing emerging outbreaks or missed targets as evidence of failure, leaders emphasized learning, adaptation, and integration. Surveillance systems were strengthened, strategies adjusted, and the limits of earlier decisions acknowledged openly. This response preserved legitimacy and prevented early success from hardening into complacency. Scale was treated as a condition to be governed, not an outcome to be declared.

A Moment of Near-Failure: Legitimizing Controlled Temperature Chain Use

One of the clearest moments when scale nearly faltered occurred early in the effort to authorize controlled temperature chain delivery. Although evidence supported the stability and safety of MenAfriVac outside the traditional cold chain, skepticism among regulators, national program managers, and frontline health workers was widespread. Cold-chain compliance functioned not only as a technical safeguard, but as a moral standard. Deviating from it risked being interpreted as lowering safety expectations for African populations rather than adapting intelligently to system constraints.

In several countries, immunization officials worried that authorizing controlled temperature chain use would expose them to professional and political risk if adverse events were reported. Frontline health workers, long disciplined for cold-chain breaches, were understandably reluctant to carry vaccines without ice packs even when formal permission existed. The risk at this juncture was therefore not simply technical failure, but erosion of trust within the delivery system itself.

Leadership intervention focused less on persuasion than on institutional protection. Global partners assumed responsibility for validating the evidence, defining temperature thresholds, and issuing unambiguous guidance that reclassified controlled temperature chain use as an approved standard rather than an exception. This buffering was decisive. By absorbing regulatory and reputational risk at higher levels of the system, leaders reduced the personal risk borne by national managers and frontline workers, making compliance feasible in practice.

In Benin, where controlled temperature chain delivery was piloted during mass campaigns, initial hesitation gave way to cautious adoption as monitoring data demonstrated feasibility and safety. Expanded reach to remote communities quickly became visible, reframing skepticism as pragmatism rather than recklessness.[7] What nearly failed at this moment was not the vaccine itself, but the legitimacy of adaptation. Leadership mattered most in transforming deviation from orthodoxy into authorized practice.

This episode illustrates a broader leadership move under scale. Evidence alone rarely resolves institutional hesitation. Scale advances when leaders intervene to realign norms, redistribute risk, and protect those expected to execute under conditions of uncertainty.

Leadership as Distributed Judgment Under Constraint

At the individual level, leadership was most visible in figures such as Marc LaForce whose role through PATH involved continuously translating epidemiological urgency and system constraints into concrete design and delivery choices. LaForce's leadership did not consist of directing national programs or enforcing compliance, but of advocating persistently for feasibility-oriented design decisions, including single-dose formulation, ultra-low pricing, and thermostability, while navigating regulatory caution and donor expectations. His influence lay in shaping what options were placed on the table and legitimized for collective consideration, rather than in controlling implementation.

At the institutional level, leadership was exercised through organizations capable of absorbing complexity and risk that could not be managed at the point of delivery. PATH functioned as a convening and buffering institution, coordinating manufacturers, funders, and technical partners while shielding frontline systems from design and regulatory complexity. The WHO played a distinct leadership role by determining whether adaptive practices, particularly controlled temperature chain use, would be authorized as legitimate standards rather than tolerated exceptions. This institutional endorsement was critical. Without it, individual national program managers and health workers would have remained exposed to professional and political risk, regardless of the strength of the evidence.

African ministries of health exercised leadership of a different kind. Rather than simply adopting externally designed solutions, they articulated the problem of epidemic meningitis as intolerable and demanded a preventive response that matched local realities. Through regional political mechanisms and policy commitments, including the Yaoundé Declaration, they generated the political momentum that made large-scale investment and coordination possible. Their leadership lay not in technical design, but in defining the problem as one requiring sustained prevention rather than episodic emergency response.

This distribution of leadership helps explain why MenAfriVac succeeded where many technically sound interventions falter. The result was not the elimination of complexity, but its deliberate redistribution in service of population-level protection.

Leadership Moves

Leadership in epidemic meningitis elimination was expressed through disciplined adaptation. Scale advanced because leaders redesigned both the intervention and its governance to function within fragile systems without eroding safety or legitimacy.

- **Redefine readiness under constraint.** Readiness was not treated as perfect procedural compliance, but as the capacity to manage risk transparently. Controlled temperature chain use reframed safety as population-level protection governed through thresholds, monitoring, and institutional accountability.
- **Redesign the intervention to fit system realities.** Leaders simplified the product so fragile systems were not forced to compensate for complexity. Single-dose formulation, ultra-low pricing, and thermostability reduced delivery burden and enabled rapid national adoption.
- **Simplify execution and shift complexity upward.** Frontline teams were asked to do fewer things well, while institutions absorbed evidence generation, regulatory justification, and reputational risk. Scale depended on deliberate decisions about where complexity should reside.
- **Centralize standards while decentralizing execution.** Global actors defined safety and evidence parameters, reducing ambiguity and shielding implementers from undue exposure. National programs retained operational control, enabling contextual adaptation without strategic fragmentation.
- **Mobilize commitment without formal authority.** Regional political leadership created sustained pressure for prevention rather than episodic crisis response. External partners aligned around shared purpose rather than hierarchical control.
- **Steward success as a dynamic condition.** Elimination of serogroup A epidemics did not end uncertainty. Leaders maintained surveillance, adapted to emerging strains, and governed success as a condition requiring ongoing recalibration, so protection could expand without compromising trust.

References

1. Rosenstein NE, Perkins BA, Stephens DS, Popovic T, Hughes JM. Meningococcal Disease. N Engl J Med. 2001 May 3;344(18):1378–88. doi:10.1056/NEJM200105033441807
2. Mazamay S, Guégan JF, Diallo N, Bompangue D, Bokabo E, Muyembe JJ, et al. An overview of bacterial meningitis epidemics in Africa from 1928 to 2018 with a focus on epidemics "outside-the-belt." BMC Infect Dis. 2021 Sep 30;21(1):1027. doi:10.1186/s12879-021-06724-1
3. Mustapha MM, Harrison LH. Vaccine prevention of meningococcal disease in Africa: major advances, remaining challenges. Hum Vaccines Immunother. 2018 May 4;14(5):1107–15. doi:10.1080/21645515.2017.1412020
4. Soeters HM, Diallo AO, Bicaba BW, Kadadé G, Dembélé AY, Acyl MA, et al. Bacterial meningitis epidemiology in five countries in the meningitis belt of sub-Saharan Africa, 2015–2017. J Infect Dis. 2019 Oct 31;220(Supplement_4):S165–74. doi:10.1093/infdis/jiz358
5. Jaca A, Wiyeh AB, Sambala EZ, Wiysonge CS. The burden of meningococcal meningitis in the African meningitis belt, from 2009 to 2014: a trend analysis. Pan Afr Med J. 2021 May 20;39(57). doi:10.11604/pamj.2021.39.57.17629
6. Lenzer J. Secret report surfaces showing that Pfizer was at fault in Nigerian drug tests. BMJ. 2006 May 25;332(7552):1233. doi:10.1136/bmj.332.7552.1233-a
7. Zipursky S, Djingarey MH, Lodjo JC, Olodo L, Tiendrebeogo S, Ronveaux O. Benefits of using vaccines out of the cold chain: delivering meningitis A vaccine in a controlled temperature chain during the mass immunization campaign in Benin. Vaccine. 2014 Mar 14;32(13):1431–5. doi:10.1016/j.vaccine.2014.01.038
8. Ezezika O, Mengistu M, Lear T. Implementation of the Meningitis Vaccine Project in Africa: lessons for vaccine implementation programs. J Glob Health Rep. 2021 Nov 2;5:e2021097. doi:10.29392/001c.29042
9. PATH. The Meningitis Vaccine Project: a groundbreaking partnership [Internet]. 2015 [cited 2026 Feb 6]. Available from: https://www.path.org/our-impact/articles/about-meningitis-vaccine-project/
10. Viviani S. Efficacy and effectiveness of the meningococcal conjugate group A vaccine MenAfriVac® in preventing recurrent meningitis epidemics in sub-Saharan Africa. Vaccines. 2022 Apr 13;10(4). doi:10.3390/vaccines10040617
11. Fernandez K, Lingani C, Aderinola OM, Goumbi K, Bicaba B, Edea ZA, et al. Meningococcal meningitis outbreaks in the African meningitis belt after meningococcal serogroup A conjugate vaccine introduction, 2011–2017. J Infect Dis. 2019 Oct 31;220(Supplement_4):S225–32. doi:10.1093/infdis/jiz355
12. Damschroder LJ, Aron DC, Keith RE, Kirsh SR, Alexander JA, Lowery JC. Fostering implementation of health services research findings into practice: a consolidated framework for advancing implementation science. Implement Sci. 2009 Aug 7;4(1):50. doi:10.1186/1748–5908-4–50
13. World Health Organization: African Region. COVID-19 threatens elimination of deadly form of meningitis in Africa, more than 50 million children miss vaccination [Internet]. 2022 [cited 2026 Feb 6]. Available from: https://www.afro.who.int/news/covid-19-threatens-elimination-deadly-form-meningitis-africa-more-50-million-children-miss
14. Trotter CL, Lingani C, Fernandez K, Cooper LV, Bita A, Tevi-Benissan C, et al. Impact of MenAfriVac in nine countries of the African meningitis belt, 2010–15: an analysis of surveillance data. Lancet Infect Dis. 2017 Aug 1;17(8):867–72. doi:10.1016/S1473–3099(17)30301-8

7 Orchestrating Decentralized Scale

Ethiopia's Health Extension Program

The Scale Challenge

Scaling primary health care in rural settings is often described as a problem of shortage. Too few clinicians, too few facilities, and too little money stand between effective interventions and population-level impact. But scarcity alone does not explain why basic services remain out of reach even when policy priorities are clear and proven interventions exist. In many low-resource settings, the deeper challenge is leadership under conditions of scale: the capacity to make consequential judgments when systems are thin, administrative reach is limited, and conventional facility-centered models of delivery cannot expand fast enough to match need.

Ethiopia confronted this dilemma directly in the early 2000s. The national question was not simply how to increase health spending or how to build clinics, but how to construct a scalable delivery model for a largely rural population with severe workforce constraints and long distances to care. The Health Extension Program emerged as a state-led strategy to solve a scale problem that could not be solved through conventional professional expansion in the near term. Rather than treating community health workers as a temporary bridge or a supplemental outreach layer, Ethiopian leaders designed a nationwide system that placed a formal, salaried community-based cadre at the center of rural primary health care delivery.[1,2] The program is often discussed as a success story of community health worker deployment. The argument in this chapter is different. The Health Extension Program is treated as a case of leadership in workforce scale and decentralized governance. Its value lies in the leadership judgments that made national expansion possible under constraint, including decisions about what to decentralize, what to standardize, what to simplify, and how to sustain political commitment long enough for a new delivery model to become institutional rather than episodic.

Ethiopia launched the Health Extension Program in 2003, with early cohorts of Health Extension Workers deployed beginning in 2004, and with rapid expansion thereafter.[1,2] Over time, evidence syntheses describe the program as contributing to improvements in service coverage and population health indicators, while also noting persistent implementation variation and emerging pressures on the frontline platform as the program matured.[3,4]

DOI: 10.4324/9781003685821-10

The scale challenge confronting leaders, therefore, was not simply how to train and deploy workers, but how to redesign a health system around a community-based platform without losing quality, legitimacy, and coherence across a diverse federal context.

Defining the Leadership Problem

The core leadership problem at the heart of Ethiopia's Health Extension Program was not "how to add more hands," but how to redefine what a functioning primary health care system looked like when professional density was low, facilities were sparse, and administrative reach was uneven. Conventional health system models assume that quality and scale flow from facilities staffed by clinicians, supported by reliable logistics, and connected by referrals. In rural Ethiopia, these assumptions were only partially true. Facility-centered expansion could not reach most households fast enough, and waiting for full system readiness would have perpetuated predictable inequities.

The leadership question, therefore, resembled the logic in the MenAfriVac project in chapter 6. Should the system be expected to transform itself to meet the requirements of conventional delivery, or should the delivery model be redesigned to fit system constraints as they existed? In Ethiopia's case, redesign implied task shifting at national scale, new role definitions, and a decision to treat community-level delivery as a core state function rather than a voluntary extension of the system.

Redesigning delivery through national-scale task shifting raised immediate legitimacy tensions. Task shifting can expand reach, but it can also be perceived as lowering standards for rural populations or asking under-supported workers to carry responsibilities without safeguards. Leaders had to make authorization decisions about scope of work, training length, supervision, and accountability. They also had to decide how to anchor Health Extension Workers institutionally so that they would be perceived as legitimate agents of the state rather than temporary project staff. Formalization mattered because scale without institutionalization becomes fragile, especially when multiple partners compete to load tasks onto the same frontline platform.[2]

A second leadership problem involved decentralization. Ethiopia's federal structure created both opportunity and risk. Local adaptation was essential, because geography, livelihoods, and social norms vary across regions. But decentralization without coherence can fragment standards and widen disparities. Empirical work on the Health Extension Program identifies substantial variation in implementation and performance across districts, indicating that national scale did not automatically translate into uniform execution.[4] Leadership was required to balance centralized purpose with decentralized operational discretion so that adaptation could occur without dissolving national accountability.

A third leadership problem involved sustaining the workforce contract over time. Scaling a cadre is not only a recruitment challenge. It becomes a retention and motivation challenge as workloads rise, expectations expand, and career pathways remain limited. Studies of Health Extension Workers document attrition and intention to leave, and they identify drivers that include working conditions, recognition, supervision, and opportunities for advancement.[5,6] Leaders had to determine whether the Health Extension Program would remain a stable foundation or become a brittle platform undermined by turnover.

The leadership problem, therefore, was one of system redesign under constraint: authorizing a new definition of acceptable primary health care delivery, governing decentralization without fragmentation, and sustaining a national workforce platform without allowing it to collapse under the weight of its own scale.

Designing for System Constraints

Redesigning Workforce Assumptions to Fit Rural Reality

One of the most consequential leadership judgments in the Health Extension Program was to redefine the workforce boundary for rural primary health care. Rather than treating rural access as a facility problem, leaders designed a new state cadre of Health Extension Workers to deliver a standardized package of services at household and community level, supported by a health post platform.[1,2] This move did not merely add workers. It reorganized rural service delivery around proximity and repeated contact, enabling prevention and behavior change to occur where people lived, rather than only when they reached facilities.

Crucially, leaders institutionalized the cadre. Health Extension Workers were positioned as government employees, rather than volunteers or temporary project staff, which signaled permanence and enabled planning at national scale.[2] This institutionalization also supported legitimacy. It clarified that community-based delivery was not a second-tier alternative, but a state-backed platform for universalizing essential services.

Leadership was also expressed through scope discipline. The Health Extension Program was structured around packages emphasizing promotive and preventive interventions and selected basic services, rather than attempting to replicate hospital or advanced clinical care at household level. This reflected a judgment about what could be executed reliably under supervision constraints, and it protected the program from becoming an unrealistic substitute for the entire health system.[1,3]

Simplifying What Had to Move Through Weak Systems

A second leadership logic involved simplifying what frontline delivery systems would be required to handle. In many scale efforts, complexity accumulates at the last mile. More indicators, more counseling messages, more reporting requirements, more vertical tasks. Ethiopia's leadership prioritized a clearly defined service package and a repeatable delivery model capable of operating across thousands of kebeles and woredas, Ethiopia's lowest administrative levels, despite limited infrastructure.[2]

This simplification was not a rejection of rigor. It was a recognition that excessive complexity produces uneven execution and weak supervision, which in turn erodes trust and performance. Evidence from district-level analyses suggests that variation in implementation quality mattered for health system performance, reinforcing the point that the challenge was not only scale-up in numbers but scale-up in consistent execution.[4]

At the same time, simplification was selective. Leaders did not simplify the stewardship responsibilities of the state. Training standards, service package definitions, and the institutional architecture of the program remained firmly national functions, even as delivery authority moved outward. In effect, complexity was not eliminated; it was repositioned. Operational tasks were decentralized, but regulatory, technical, and normative oversight were deliberately concentrated at higher levels of the system—where institutional capacity to manage standards and ensure accountability was stronger.

This redistribution of complexity laid the foundation for a second, equally important, leadership move.

Centralizing Standards While Decentralizing Action

A complementary leadership move involved separating authority over standards from authority over execution. National and central authorities maintained a coherent logic of the Health Extension Program, including core packages, training expectations, and the health post as the delivery platform, while regional and district systems adapted implementation to context.[2] This balance was essential. Without standardization, scale could fragment into local variants that undermine equity. Without local discretion, the program could fail operationally in settings where geographic, cultural, and administrative conditions vary sharply.

Empirical research on the Health Extension Program shows both the value and the difficulty of this balance. District performance variation indicates that decentralization created space for strong districts to do well, while also allowing weak districts to lag, especially where supervision and supply systems were limited.[4] Leadership, therefore, was not only designing the initial balance, but continuously recalibrating it as disparities emerged.

Mobilizing Community Participation Without Diluting Accountability

Ethiopia's Health Extension Program relied on community participation not as a peripheral communication strategy, but as a core mechanism for achieving scale. Leaders recognized that even a nationally deployed cadre of Health Extension Workers could not alone generate the frequency of contact and social reinforcement required to change household behaviors. The program therefore built a structured diffusion system that extended beyond the health post, using model households and organized community networks to embed health practices into everyday life. Empirical analyses consistently identify this architecture of participation as central to the program's reach and uptake, particularly for maternal, child, and preventive health behaviors.[1,3] Studies from rural southern Ethiopia link structured community participation under Health Extension Worker supervision with increased utilization of maternal health services, illustrating how participation functioned as a diffusion mechanism rather than a substitute for service delivery.[7]

This strategy, however, introduced a leadership tension that required careful governance. Community mobilization can expand reach, but it can also dilute accountability if responsibility shifts informally from the state to households and volunteers without adequate support. Evidence from Ethiopia's Women's Development Army illustrates this risk. Volunteer networks increased participation and visibility, but they also exposed disparities in motivation, recognition, and burden, particularly among women expected to contribute unpaid labor under social pressure.[8,9] Left unmanaged, such dynamics risked turning community engagement into a substitute for state responsibility rather than a complement to it.

Leadership responded by preserving a clear accountability spine. Health Extension Workers remained the formal, salaried agents of the state, responsible for technical delivery, prioritization, and linkage to the health system. Community structures functioned as force multipliers, reinforcing adoption and trust, but not as replacements for public provision. This distinction mattered. It ensured that scale was achieved through social diffusion without eroding public responsibility for quality, equity, and continuity of care. Community participation strengthened scale precisely because it was governed, not romanticized.

Sustaining Momentum Through Reform and Workforce Stewardship

As the Health Extension Program matured, the leadership challenge shifted from expansion and community participation to stewardship. Calls from within Ethiopia's public health community emphasize that the program's continued relevance depends on active governance, adaptation, and reform rather than reliance on past achievements.[10] A scaled frontline platform inevitably attracts demand. New health priorities, donor-funded initiatives, reporting requirements, and community expectations accumulate on the same cadre and the same delivery node. Without disciplined governance, this produces overload rather than impact. Recent reform roadmaps acknowledge this explicitly, emphasizing the need to optimize the program for quality, time use, and evolving disease burdens, particularly as non-communicable conditions rise alongside persistent infectious risks.[11]

Evidence from workforce studies clarifies why stewardship is decisive at scale. Attrition and intention to leave among Health Extension Workers are shaped less by initial training than by working conditions, recognition, supervision quality, and opportunities for progression. National and regional analyses document rising attrition over time and significant variation across contexts, underscoring that scale does not stabilize itself.[5,6] When workload expands faster than support systems, a platform can hollow out quietly, maintaining coverage on paper while execution and morale erode.

Leadership under these conditions requires protecting the workforce contract as actively as expanding the workforce itself. Reform efforts in Ethiopia increasingly focus on strengthening supervision, clarifying scope, improving efficiency, and aligning expectations with capacity. These are not technical afterthoughts. They are the core leadership work of sustaining scale. The Health Extension Program's durability depends not on how many workers were deployed, but on whether leaders continue to govern the platform as a living system rather than a completed achievement.

Tensions and Trade-Offs

Leadership under conditions of scale required continuous navigation of tensions that could not be resolved once and for all. These tensions were not incidental. They were constitutive of the leadership challenge.

The first tension lay between reach and quality. Rapid workforce expansion dramatically increased access, but quality depended on training depth, supportive supervision, commodity availability, and referral functionality. Ethiopia's leadership strategy managed this tension through scope discipline and standardized service packages, but implementation variation remained visible at district level, indicating that quality could not be fully built into the initial scale design.[4] Evidence from health post readiness assessments shows that infrastructure, supplies, and perceived preparedness of Health Extension Workers varied substantially across regions, underscoring how quality at scale remained contingent on local context rather than uniform platform design.[12] Leaders therefore faced a recurring judgment: how much quality to embed upfront and how much to strengthen iteratively without eroding legitimacy or slowing expansion.

A second tension involved standardization versus contextual adaptation. Scale favors standardization because it simplifies training, supervision, and accountability. Yet Ethiopia's geographic, cultural, and administrative diversity made rigid uniformity operationally unrealistic. Evidence of interregional disparities in implementation underscores the limits of one-size-fits-all delivery and the need for differentiated support.[13] The leadership challenge was not whether to adapt, but how to permit adaptation without producing fragmentation or inequity across a federal system.

The third tension centered on decentralization versus accountability. Decentralization enabled responsiveness and local problem-solving, but it also risked diffusing responsibility as the frontline platform accumulated multiple programs and reporting demands. Urban and rural implementation studies document coordination challenges, workload pressures, and experience gaps as the Health Extension Program evolved into a multipurpose delivery platform.[14] Leaders had to decide where accountability should ultimately reside and how to preserve clarity of purpose as the platform became increasingly congested.

Together, these tensions reinforce a central claim of Part II. Leadership at scale is not about choosing a clean solution. It is about managing trade-offs over time, preserving legitimacy while sustaining execution.

What Scaled and What Nearly Failed

The Health Extension Program achieved national scale in both workforce and platform terms. It established a standardized delivery node, the health post, and embedded a salaried state cadre of Health Extension Workers close to households across rural Ethiopia. Evidence syntheses associate the program with improvements in access, service coverage, and community health practices, while also noting emerging pressures as expectations expanded.[1,3]

What scaled was not only personnel. What scaled was an institutional arrangement. Ethiopia expanded a model of state presence at community level that did not depend on near-term physician density expansion. This institutionalization, rather than the sheer number of workers deployed, explains why the program became a reference point for countries seeking to scale community health systems under severe workforce constraints. Economic evaluations of the Health Extension Program further reinforce this logic, showing that several standardized service packages deliver favorable value relative to cost, strengthening the case for scale through a defined package rather than unchecked scope expansion.[15]

At the same time, scale exposed fragility. District and regional variation revealed uneven implementation capacity and disparities in service quality.[4,13] Urban adaptation introduced new coordination and engagement challenges that did not mirror rural settings.[14] Most importantly, scale placed sustained pressure on the workforce contract. Longitudinal evidence shows that attrition and intention to leave increased as workloads expanded faster than supervision, recognition, and career pathways.[5,6] Scale succeeded in building reach, but it also created conditions under which the platform itself could quietly weaken.

This is where leadership became most visible. Not at the moment of launch, but at the moment when a scaled platform risked overload and legitimacy erosion.

A Moment of Near-Failure: When Scale Began to Outrun Support

Ethiopia's near-failure moment of system overload was not a single dramatic breakdown. It took a more common and more dangerous form. The platform became so valuable that it was asked to carry more than it could sustain.

As the Health Extension Program matured, it increasingly functioned as the default channel for multiple health priorities. Tasks, reporting requirements, and expectations accumulated, even where supervision capacity, supply reliability, and referral systems remained uneven. Implementation studies highlight how workload, coordination complexity, and contextual mismatch shaped frontline experience, particularly in urban settings.[14] Workforce research further indicates that motivation and retention became material threats to sustainability as demands outpaced support.[5,6]

The leadership risk at this point was not collapse but hollowing out. Coverage would persist on paper while execution weakened, morale eroded, and community trust became inconsistent. When that happens, the state's legitimacy at household level begins to fray.

Leadership responses focused on reform and optimization rather than expansion. National roadmaps emphasized improving quality, protecting time use, strengthening supervision, and recalibrating the program for evolving disease burdens.[11] This near-failure moment clarifies a transferable lesson. Workforce scale is not protected by recruitment alone. It is protected by governance discipline, scope control, and sustained investment in the workforce contract.

Leadership Decisions under Constraint

The Health Extension Program did not scale through a single decree or centralized authority. It scaled through distributed leadership judgments across national, regional, and local levels about what should be standardized, what could be delegated, and what had to be simplified.

National leadership established the program's core logic by institutionalizing Health Extension Workers as a state cadre and anchoring delivery in standardized health posts.[1,2] Regional and district leadership shaped implementation under diverse conditions, explaining observed performance variation and the need for targeted strengthening.[4] Community-level engagement converted a delivery platform into sustained household uptake, a feature consistently emphasized in program syntheses.[3]

This distribution of leadership also explains why sustainability depends on continued governance. A scaled frontline platform cannot remain stable if authority fragments, tasks proliferate without discipline, and workforce stewardship is neglected. Leadership at scale is less about launching programs than about keeping them coherent under strain.

Leadership Moves

Leadership in scaling Ethiopia's community health system was not expressed through technical novelty or flawless execution. It was expressed through deliberate moves that enabled action at national scale despite scarce professionals, uneven infrastructure, and persistent pressure to overload the frontline platform.

- **Redefine readiness under constraint.** Rather than treating physician density, facility coverage, or referral completeness as prerequisites for expansion, leaders authorized a community-based delivery model as a legitimate core of the health system. This shift moved the system from aspirational readiness to functional adequacy and allowed national scale to proceed without waiting for ideal conditions.
- **Institutionalize task shifting within state architecture.** Health Extension Workers were formalized as a salaried government cadre with defined roles, training, and scope. Embedding task shifting in government structures protected legitimacy and accountability at scale and prevented community-based delivery from being dismissed as volunteerism or temporary outreach.
- **Protect the frontline platform from overload.** As new priorities, donors, and reporting demands accumulated, leaders resisted turning Health Extension Workers into an all-purpose solution. Scope discipline required saying no to additional tasks unless supervision, supplies, and support systems could keep pace.

- **Centralize standards while governing decentralization.** National authorities defined purpose, service packages, and training expectations, while regional and district actors adapted execution. When disparities emerged, leaders responded with targeted correction rather than recentralization, preserving coherence without collapsing local discretion.
- **Mobilize community participation without diluting accountability.** Model households and community networks extended the reach of Health Extension Workers and reinforced household-level adoption. Leaders preserved legitimacy by keeping Health Extension Workers as the formal agents of the state, ensuring that participation strengthened public responsibility rather than replacing it.
- **Shift from expansion to stewardship before erosion is visible.** As signs of overload, attrition, and declining morale appeared, leadership attention moved toward workforce sustainability, supervision quality, and platform optimization. Treating scale as a condition requiring maintenance prevented quiet decline from hardening into systemic fragility.

References

1. Banteyerga H. Ethiopia's Health Extension Program: improving health through community involvement. MEDICC Rev. 2011 Jul;13(3):46–9.
2. Workie NW, Ramana GN. Ethiopia – The Health Extension Program in Ethiopia [Internet]. Washington, DC: The World Bank; 2013 Jan p. 34. (UNICO Studies Series 10). Report No.: 74963. Available from: https://documents.worldbank.org/en/publication/documents-reports/documentdetail/356621468032070256
3. Assefa Y, Gelaw YA, Hill PS, Taye BW, Van Damme W. Community Health Extension Program of Ethiopia, 2003–2018: successes and challenges toward universal coverage for primary healthcare services. Global Health. 2019 Mar 26;15(1):24.
4. Fetene N, Linnander E, Fekadu B, Alemu H, Omer H, Canavan M, et al. The Ethiopian Health Extension Program and variation in health systems performance: what matters? PLOS ONE. 2016 May 26;11(5):e0156438.
5. Tekle MG, Wolde HM, Medhin G, Teklu AM, Alemayehu YK, Gebre EG, et al. Understanding the factors affecting attrition and intention to leave of health extension workers: a mixed methods study in Ethiopia. Hum Resour Health. 2022 Feb 19;20(1):20.
6. Wolde HM, Tekle MG, Alemayehu YK, Gebre EG, Teklu AM. Attrition of health extension workers in Ethiopia: trends, regional variations and determinants – a mixed methods study of 15 years of experience. BMC Health Serv Res. 2023 Dec 20;23(1):1444.
7. Datiko DG, Bunte EM, Birrie GB, Kea AZ, Steege R, Taegtmeyer M, et al. Community participation and maternal health service utilization: lessons from the Health Extension Programme in rural southern Ethiopia. Journal of Global Health Reports [Internet]. 2019 Apr 1 [cited 2026 Feb 17];3. Available from: https://www.joghr.org/article/11978-community-participation-and-maternal-health-service-utilization-lessons-from-the-health-extension-programme-in-rural-southern-ethiopia
8. Maes K, Closser S, Tesfaye Y, Gilbert Y, Abesha R. Volunteers in Ethiopia's women's development army are more deprived and distressed than their neighbors: cross-sectional survey data from rural Ethiopia. BMC Public Health. 2018 Feb 14;18(1):258.
9. Closser S, Napier H, Maes K, Abesha R, Gebremariam H, Backe G, et al. Does volunteer community health work empower women? Evidence from Ethiopia's Women's Development Army. Health Policy Plan. 2019 May 1;34(4):298–306.

10. Haileamlak A. Editorial message. Ethiopian Journal of Health Sciences [Internet]. 2023 Jan 1 [cited 2026 Feb 14];33(1). Available from: https://www.ajol.info/index.php/ejhs/article/view/244581
11. Tesema AG, Peiris D, Joshi R, Abimbola S, Fentaye FW, Teklu AM, et al. Exploring complementary and competitive relations between non-communicable disease services and other Health Extension Programme services in Ethiopia: a multilevel analysis. BMJ Glob Health [Internet]. 2022 Jun 23 [cited 2026 Feb 14];7(6). Available from: https://gh.bmj.com/content/7/6/e009025
12. Getachew T, Abebe SM, Yitayal M, Bergström A, Persson LA, Berhanu D. Health extension workers' perceived health system context and health post preparedness to provide services: a cross-sectional study in four Ethiopian regions. BMJ Open. 2021 Jun 1;11(6):e048517.
13. Haregu TN, Alemayehu YK, Alemu YA, Medhin G, Woldegiorgis MA, Fentaye FW, et al. Disparities in the implementation of the Health Extension Program in Ethiopia: doing more and better towards universal health coverage. Dialogues Health. 2022 Dec;1:100047.
14. Zebre G, Gizaw AT, Tareke KG, Lemu YK. Implementation, experience, and challenges of urban Health Extension Program in Addis Ababa: a case study from Ethiopia. BMC Public Health. 2021 Jan 19;21(1):167.
15. Assebe LF, Belete WN, Alemayehu S, Asfaw E, Godana KT, Alemayehu YK, et al. Economic evaluation of Health Extension Program packages in Ethiopia. PLOS ONE. 2021 Feb 2;16(2):e0246207.

8 Governing Speed and Legitimacy

COVID-19 Vaccine Rollout

The Scale Challenge

By late 2020, the world faced a paradox. Vaccines had been developed at unprecedented speed, yet population protection remained uncertain. The question was no longer whether science could move quickly. It was whether governance could keep pace. COVID-19 vaccine scale-up was not primarily a scientific story. It was a leadership story. Leaders were required to authorize, finance, manufacture, allocate, and deliver simultaneously, while evidence evolved and public scrutiny intensified. New platforms, rapid trials, and unprecedented manufacturing output created the impression that the central scale problem had been solved by innovation. The argument in this chapter is different. COVID-19 vaccine scale-up is treated as a case of leadership under conditions of scale. It required consequential judgments when systems were stressed, governance authority was fragmented, supply was structurally unequal, and public trust was contested.

The challenge was not only to develop vaccines quickly, but to make population protection possible while the pandemic was still unfolding. Unlike eradication campaigns or planned introductions like MenAfriVac, leaders were asked to authorize, finance, manufacture, allocate, and deliver at the same time. They also had to explain shifting evidence and policy reversals under intense public scrutiny.

By 2022, global vaccine administration reached billions of doses, reflecting the largest immunization effort in history, with data compiled and updated through global reporting systems.[1,2] Yet the distribution of protection was uneven. Early access was concentrated in high-income countries, while many low-income countries experienced delayed supply and episodic delivery.[3,4]

The scale challenge confronting leaders was therefore not simply how to deliver vaccines. It was how to govern speed without losing legitimacy, coordinate across borders without enforcement power, and sustain uptake in settings where misinformation and politicization undermined institutional credibility.

Leadership Problem Definition

The core leadership problem at the heart of COVID-19 vaccine scale-up was not how to produce vaccines quickly, but how to authorize and govern population-level

DOI: 10.4324/9781003685821-11

action when conventional sequencing was no longer viable. Established models of vaccine development assume a progression from evidence generation to regulatory approval, followed by manufacturing scale-up and delivery through relatively stable immunization systems. During COVID-19, this progression could not be preserved without accepting catastrophic delay. In late 2020, delay did not mean inconvenience; it meant preventable deaths accumulating daily while hospitals and health workforces were already breaking.

Leaders therefore faced a foundational judgment about what constituted acceptable decision-making under emergency conditions. The question was not whether scientific uncertainty existed, but whether waiting for its resolution was compatible with protecting populations during an active pandemic. This required redefining readiness from a state of completion to a state of managed risk, supported by surveillance, adaptive policy, and ongoing evidence generation.[5,6]

A second leadership problem involved governing action across fragmented authority. No global institution possessed the mandate or enforcement power to allocate vaccines equitably across countries. At the same time, national governments remained politically accountable for domestic outcomes. Leaders had to operate within this structural reality, designing coordination mechanisms that could influence behavior without overriding national sovereignty.[7]

A third leadership problem concerned sustaining public uptake under conditions of visible uncertainty and politicization. Vaccine scale required not only logistics and supply, but continued consent. Leaders were required to make policy adjustments in public, revise guidance as evidence evolved, and communicate risk in ways that preserved institutional credibility.

Taken together, the leadership problem in COVID-19 vaccine scale-up was one of governing action without the stabilizing conditions normally assumed in large-scale public health programs. Leaders were required to authorize action early, coordinate without central authority, and sustain legitimacy while policies evolved in real time.

Designing for System Constraints

Redesigning Governance Assumptions to Fit Emergency Reality

One of the most consequential leadership judgments was to abandon sequential governance in favor of overlapping processes. In the United States, Operation Warp Speed formalized this approach by investing in development, manufacturing, and distribution planning in parallel, accepting that some candidates would fail.[6] This was not primarily a technical decision. It was a governance decision to shift risk forward in time. The US Department of Health and Human Services described the distribution challenge as requiring adaptive allocation and nimble delivery strategies because demand, supply, and logistics would change rapidly.[8]

Regulators in multiple jurisdictions adopted emergency pathways, but the United Kingdom's decision on December 2, 2020, illustrates the leadership stakes. By authorizing the Pfizer–BioNTech vaccine ahead of the European Medicines

Agency, the UK government accepted institutional and political risk in exchange for speed.[9] In the United States, the Food and Drug Administration issued an Emergency Use Authorization for the Pfizer-BioNTech vaccine on December 11, 2020 and for Moderna on December 18, 2020.[5,10] These decisions institutionalized a new operational definition of readiness: readiness meant a risk profile judged acceptable under emergency conditions, not a fully matured evidence base.

This redesign resembles the logic seen in smallpox eradication. Leaders did not wait for perfect systems. They revised what "good enough to act" meant, then built learning and correction into execution.

Simplifying What Had to Move Through Weak and Stressed Systems

A second leadership logic involved simplifying what delivery systems were asked to manage while complexity was redistributed upward to institutions better able to carry it. During COVID-19, the last mile was asked to deliver adult vaccination at scale, often with limited adult immunization infrastructure and health workforces already stretched by crisis response.

Leaders responded with delivery simplification through temporary platforms. Mass clinics, pop-up sites, mobile units, and pharmacy-based channels expanded capacity quickly. This was analogous to earlier scale efforts in which emergency campaigns were used to achieve rapid reach, with system integration deferred.

At the same time, complexity increased in upstream systems. Cold-chain requirements for mRNA vaccines created operational barriers, particularly in low-resource settings. Leaders in countries with strong digital and primary care infrastructure, such as Chile and Israel, were able to convert supply into rapid uptake using centralized registries and clear prioritization. In other settings, delivery capacity was constrained not only by infrastructure but also by governance coherence and trust.

Centralizing Standards While Decentralizing Action

A complementary leadership move involved separating authority over standards from authority over execution. The World Health Organization (WHO) issued prioritization guidance and a structured roadmap for vaccine use during limited supply, emphasizing phased prioritization by risk and exposure.[11] National governments translated these recommendations into local priority groups and delivery models based on epidemiology, supply, and political context.

This balance created persistent variation. Some variation was functional. It allowed adaptation to different workforce capabilities, geography, and risk profiles. But variation also exposed inequities, especially where supply constraints were structural rather than temporary.

Mobilizing Global Coordination Without Diluting National Accountability

COVID-19 vaccine scale-up required coordination mechanisms that could operate without a global government. The Access to COVID-19 Tools Accelerator was created to organize diagnostics, therapeutics, vaccines, and health systems support, with WHO playing key roles across pillars and allocation workstreams.[12] Within this architecture, COVAX was co-led by CEPI, Gavi, and WHO, with UNICEF as a key delivery partner, and with regional procurement arrangements such as the PAHO Revolving Fund in the Americas.[7] As subsequent analyses of the COVID-19 vaccine response make clear, these hybrid arrangements were not design failures but reflections of a deeper leadership constraint: global coordination mechanisms lacked the authority to override national procurement decisions, leaving equity dependent on voluntary cooperation rather than enforceable governance.[13]

The leadership promise of COVAX was pooled procurement and equity. Its operational reality was hybrid. Countries continued bilateral purchasing, often absorbing early supply, while COVAX sought to provide a parallel channel for global access.[7] COVAX achieved large-scale delivery over time, including more than 1.8 billion doses and related delivery supplies, with substantial reach across lower-income economies.[14]

The fragility of this architecture became visible in March 2021, when export restrictions from India's Serum Institute disrupted expected COVAX shipments.[15,16] Countries planning national rollouts suddenly faced uncertainty not of their own making. Reuters reporting documented how export curbs and delays affected expected COVAX deliveries in early 2021, with downstream impacts on countries planning their rollouts.[15,16] This illustrates a leadership constraint at scale: even strong coordination mechanisms can be undermined when manufacturing is concentrated and national crisis pressures reshape export decisions.

Sustaining Momentum Through Adaptation, Boosters, and Trust Stewardship

As rollout progressed, leadership challenges shifted from initial access to sustained protection under variant pressure. Leaders faced uncertainty about durability, variant escape, and the timing and targeting of boosters. These were not only technical decisions. They were distributive, legitimacy decisions because booster policies in high-income countries had direct implications for global supply and perceived fairness.

The equity tension became explicit in August 2021, when WHO called for a temporary moratorium on booster doses to prioritize primary vaccination in low-income countries. The request was not merely technical; it was distributive. Booster campaigns in high-income countries signaled protection at home while first doses remained unavailable elsewhere.[17] Even where boosters were epidemiologically justified, the governance optics mattered. Leaders had to choose between domestic pressure for expanded protection and global arguments for fairness and epidemic control.

Trust stewardship became decisive. In settings where policy changes were communicated as evidence-based updates, the public could tolerate revisions. Where policy reversals were framed politically or inconsistently, trust eroded. Trust was therefore not simply a communication outcome. It was a byproduct of institutional coherence: the visible alignment of evidence, policy authority, accountability, and explanation. The leadership task was not to eliminate uncertainty, but to govern it transparently.

Tensions and Trade-Offs

Leadership under conditions of scale required continuous navigation of tensions that could not be resolved once and for all.

The first tension was speed versus certainty. Emergency authorization compressed timelines dramatically, enabling early protection, but it required ongoing surveillance and periodic policy revision.[5,10]

The second tension was nationalism versus solidarity. National procurement enabled rapid domestic deployment, but it constrained early global access and created dependency on donations and delayed COVAX supply.[7,15]

The third tension was innovation versus readiness. mRNA vaccines were scientifically powerful, but the logistics requirements increased delivery complexity. Leaders had to decide whether to retrofit systems to technology or prioritize easier-to-deploy platforms in settings with constrained infrastructure.

The fourth tension was communication versus governance. Vaccine hesitancy was often treated as a communication deficit, yet many failures were governance failures. Conflicting messages, shifting definitions of "fully vaccinated," and politicized mandates produced resistance in some settings even when vaccines were available.

These tensions are summarized in Table 8.1, which frames COVID-19 vaccine scale-up as a sequence of leadership judgments rather than a single technical pathway.

Table 8.1 Leadership Decisions Under Constraint in COVID-19 Vaccine Scale-Up

Constraint	*Technically Plausible Response*	*Leadership Decision*	*Contribution to Scale*
1. Extreme time pressure and global crisis conditions	Sequential clinical, regulatory, and deployment processes	Overlapping development, authorization, and rollout under emergency frameworks	Compressed timelines dramatically, enabling vaccine availability within months rather than years
2. Fragmented global governance and national self-interest	Reliance on voluntary international coordination alone	Combination of national procurement strategies with selective multilateral mechanisms	Enabled rapid domestic deployment while sustaining partial global coordination
3. Profound uncertainty about variants, durability, and supply	Delayed rollout pending complete evidence	Action under uncertainty, with adaptive policy and continuous evidence updating	Allowed early population protection despite evolving scientific knowledge

(*Continued*)

Table 8.1 (Continued)

Constraint	*Technically Plausible Response*	*Leadership Decision*	*Contribution to Scale*
4. Highly unequal manufacturing and supply capacity	Market-driven allocation based on purchasing power	Advance purchase agreements, technology transfer, and pooled procurement initiatives	Expanded production capacity and moderated, though did not eliminate, global inequities
5. Public mistrust, misinformation, and politicization	Uniform risk communication based on technical evidence	Context-specific communication strategies and engagement with trusted intermediaries	Improved uptake in some settings by aligning messages with social and political realities
6. Risk of bypassing or overwhelming health systems	Creation of permanent parallel delivery infrastructures	Use of temporary delivery platforms alongside selective system integration	Enabled rapid rollout while limiting long-term disruption to routine health services

What Scaled and What Nearly Failed

What scaled was not only the product. What scaled was an institutional arrangement that accepted emergency governance as legitimate. Emergency authorizations, at-risk manufacturing, and parallel delivery platforms made population protection possible at unprecedented speed.[6,10] Global reporting shows the resulting expansion in administered doses and coverage over time.[1,2]

Yet the near-failure moment was not a single breakdown. It was the convergence of inequity, supply shocks, and trust erosion. In many low-income countries, early scale depended on delayed shipments and unpredictable delivery schedules, which made planning difficult and undermined public confidence in availability. Supply disruptions linked to export constraints highlighted how dependent equity was on a small number of manufacturing nodes.[15,16] These inequities were not accidental implementation failures. They were structured by manufacturing concentration, advance purchase agreements, export restrictions, and unequal purchasing power. Country-level evidence also shows that inequity was experienced through practical implementation barriers, including access constraints, uneven outreach, language gaps, and weak accountability in vaccine allocation.[18] In high-income countries, policy shifts and politicized debates over mandates risked turning scientific uncertainty into institutional distrust. These dynamics threatened not only COVID-19 coverage but also broader confidence in immunization systems.

As with smallpox, the deeper objective was not coverage alone but institutional durability. Scale that erodes legitimacy ultimately undermines itself.

Leadership Moves

Leadership in COVID-19 vaccine scale was not expressed through a single global plan. It emerged through deliberate moves that enabled action at speed while preserving legitimacy under strain.

- **Redefine readiness under uncertainty.** Readiness was treated not as evidentiary closure but as a risk profile judged acceptable under emergency conditions. Acting early required institutional commitment to surveillance, transparency, and iterative policy revision rather than waiting for complete evidence while mortality accumulated.
- **Design governance that reflects political reality.** Hybrid arrangements combining national procurement with partial multilateral coordination acknowledged the limits of global enforcement authority. Imperfect coordination enabled movement where idealized models of centralized allocation would have stalled.
- **Simplify execution and shift complexity upward.** Temporary delivery platforms and clear prioritization frameworks reduced the burden on last-mile systems, while regulatory interpretation, supply forecasting, and risk management were concentrated in institutions better positioned to manage uncertainty and oversight.
- **Treat inequity as a structural constraint.** Manufacturing concentration and purchasing power predictably shaped early access. Anticipating these distortions and embedding corrective mechanisms in procurement, allocation, and dose-sharing decisions proved more effective than relying on downstream redistribution.
- **Govern trust as an institutional function.** Policy revision, booster recalibration, and shifting eligibility criteria were inevitable under evolving evidence. Legitimacy depended on consistent rationale, clear accountability, and visible alignment between scientific guidance and political authority.
- **Shift from expansion to stewardship before strain becomes visible.** Rapid rollout generated quiet pressures on supply chains, health workforces, and public confidence. Leaders had to recalibrate early, protect core systems, and avoid adding new demands in ways that allowed urgency to harden into institutional erosion.

References

1. Mathieu E, Ritchie H, Rodés-Guirao L, Appel C, Gavrilov D, Giattino C, et al. Coronavirus (COVID-19) vaccinations. Our World in Data [Internet]. 2020 Dec 16 [cited 2026 Feb 10]; Available from: https://ourworldindata.org/covid-vaccinations
2. World Health Organization. COVID-19 vaccines | WHO COVID-19 dashboard [Internet]. World Health Organization Datadot. World Health Organization; 2024 [cited 2026 Feb 10]. Available from: https://data.who.int/dashboards/covid19/vaccines

3. World Health Organization. WHO SAGE roadmap for prioritizing uses of COVID-19 vaccines in the context of limited supply: an approach to inform planning and subsequent recommendations based on epidemiological setting and vaccine supply scenarios, first issued 20 October 2020, latest update 16 July 2021 [Internet]. World Health Organization; 2021 [cited 2026 Feb 10]. Available from: https://iris.who.int/items/f47b3190-d4ed-489e-b74c-4d972a12b955
4. World Health Organization. WHO SAGE roadmap for prioritizing uses of COVID-19 vaccines: an approach to optimize the global impact of COVID-19 vaccines, based on public health goals, global and national equity, and vaccine access and coverage scenarios [Internet]. World Health Organization; 2023 [cited 2026 Feb 10]. Available from: https://www.who.int/publications/i/item/WHO-2019-nCoV-Vaccines-SAGE-Prioritization-2023.1
5. Food and Drug Administration. Pfizer-BioNTech COVID-19 vaccine EUA letter of authorization [Internet]. Food and Drug Administration; 2021. Available from: https://www.fda.gov/media/144412/download
6. Van Norman GA. "Warp speed" operations in the COVID-19 pandemic. JACC Basic Transl Sci. 2020 Jun 17;5(7):730–4.
7. World Health Organization. COVAX [Internet]. World Health Organization; 2022 [cited 2026 Feb 10]. Available from: https://www.who.int/initiatives/act-accelerator/covax
8. U.S. Department of Health and Human Sciences. From the factory to the frontlines. U.S. Department of Health and Human Sciences; p. 1–11.
9. Department of Health and Social Care. UK authorises Pfizer/BioNTech COVID-19 vaccine [Internet]. GOV.UK. Department of Health and Social Care; 2020 [cited 2026 Feb 10]. Available from: https://www.gov.uk/government/news/uk-authorises-pfizer-biontech-covid-19-vaccine
10. Department of Health and Human Sevices, Food and Drug Administration. Authorizations of emergency use of two biological products during the COVID-19 pandemic; availability [Internet]. Federal Register. Food and Drug Administration, HHS.; 2021 [cited 2026 Feb 10]. Available from: https://www.federalregister.gov/documents/2021/01/19/2021-01022/authorizations-of-emergency-use-of-two-biological-products-during-the-covid-19-pandemic-availability
11. World Health Organization. WHO SAGE roadmap for prioritizing uses of COVID-19 vaccines in the context of limited supply: an approach to inform planning and subsequent recommendations based upon epidemiologic setting and vaccine supply scenarios, 20 October 2020 [Internet]. World Health Organization; 2020 [cited 2026 Feb 10]. Available from: https://iris.who.int/items/e7040066-b679-4b9c-8dba-34f1afa2cccf
12. World Health Organization. What is the ACT accelerator [Internet]. World Health Organization; 2022 [cited 2026 Feb 10]. Available from: https://www.who.int/initiatives/act-accelerator/about
13. Moon S, Ruiz AA, Vieira M. Averting future vaccine injustice. New England Journal of Medicine. 2021 Jul 14;385(3):193–6.
14. Gavi The Vaccine Alliance. COVAX facility [Internet]. Gavi The Vaccine Alliance. Gavi; 2026 [cited 2026 Feb 10]. Available from: https://www.gavi.org/covax-facility
15. Das K. EXCLUSIVE India delays big exports of AstraZeneca shot, as infections surge | Reuters [Internet]. Reuters; 2021 [cited 2026 Feb 10]. Available from: https://www.reuters.com/business/healthcare-pharmaceuticals/exclusive-india-delays-big-exports-astrazeneca-shot-infections-surge-2021-03-25/
16. Morales NJ, Cha S. Asian countries seek vaccine supplies after India export curbs hit COVAX [Internet]. 2021 Mar 30 [cited 2026 Feb 10]. Available from: https://www.reuters.com/business/healthcare-pharmaceuticals/asian-countries-scramble-vaccine-supplies-after-india-export-curbs-2021-03-30/

17. Mishra M, Nadeem D. WHO calls for halting COVID-19 vaccine boosters in favor of unvaccinated [Internet]. 2021 Aug 4 [cited 2026 Feb 10]; Available from: https://www.reuters.com/business/healthcare-pharmaceuticals/who-calls-moratorium-covid-19-vaccine-booster-doses-until-september-end-2021-08-04/
18. Okolie A, Rahman S, Kothari A, Ezezika O. What are the key determinants to fostering equity within coronavirus disease 2019 (COVID-19) vaccination deployment initiatives in Nigeria? A scoping review. Global Health Journal. 2025 Mar 1;9.

Part III

Governing for Durable Scale

The earlier parts of this book established that scaling health interventions is not primarily a technical challenge, but a leadership one. The case studies in Part II showed this in practice: as interventions expanded, authority fragmented, incentives diverged, uncertainty persisted, and legitimacy had to be actively maintained. Part III turns from examining leadership under constraint in practice to the question of how scale endures once interventions enter routine systems and confront structural constraint.

Durability introduces a different set of pressures. Early expansion can generate visibility, political momentum, and concentrated resources. Over time, however, incentives shift, attention diffuses, financing tightens, and institutional fatigue emerges. Performance depends less on technical design alone and more on whether leaders can sustain alignment across actors who retain autonomy and whose interests are only partially shared. The central task becomes governance under conditions of dispersion rather than mobilization under conditions of urgency.

This section examines three recurring forms of leadership work that determine whether scale holds. The first concerns stakeholder alignment and coalition management: how leaders stabilize cooperation among actors with unequal power, competing mandates, and uneven trust. The second concerns financing and resource mobilization: how funding arrangements embed obligation, distribute risk, and shape long-term durability. The third concerns innovation, adaptation, and continuous learning: how leaders design feedback mechanisms and authorize recalibration so that systems respond to strain without fracturing.

The purpose of this section is conceptual rather than illustrative. It names the recurring pressures that emerge once scale expands and clarifies the decisions leaders must make when legitimacy is uneven, resources are constrained, and coordination is distributed across levels of governance. Together, these chapters argue that scale is not a completed achievement. It is a condition that must be governed and renewed through alignment, stewardship, and disciplined adaptation as contexts evolve.

DOI: 10.4324/9781003685821-12

9 Aligning Stakeholders and Governing Coalitions

Coalitions, Power, and Alignment in Health Scale-Up

Scaling health innovations is rarely constrained by a lack of evidence or technical feasibility; rather, it is constrained by whether systems, relationships, and incentives can be aligned long enough for scale to take hold. This is where leadership enters, not as vision alone, but as the sustained work of alignment under real-world conditions. Across global health, the dominant narrative often assumes that once an intervention has been shown to be effective, the primary challenge is one of replication: expanding coverage, standardizing delivery, and mobilizing sufficient resources. Yet decades of experience in low- and middle-income countries (LMICs) suggest that this assumption is deeply flawed. Interventions stall, fracture, or collapse, not because the science is weak, but because the social, political, and institutional environments required to sustain scale are insufficiently aligned.[1,2]

Stakeholder engagement and coalition-building sit at the heart of this challenge.[3,4] Scale is not achieved by single organizations acting in isolation, nor by heroic leaders pushing innovations through resistant systems. It is achieved through coalitions that bring together actors with divergent interests, unequal power, and differing levels of trust, and that hold long enough for systems to adapt. These coalitions must navigate political authority, cultural legitimacy, historical memory, and resource competition, all while maintaining momentum under conditions of uncertainty.

The reflections in this chapter draw directly on my experience working alongside governments, implementing partners, and international agencies on health scale-up efforts, as well as on qualitative interviews and comparative case analyses reported in my previously published work and synthesized in *Scaling Up Health Innovations in Africa*.[5] Revisiting the cases and interviews from that work, I was struck by how consistently scale hinged less on technical design than on whether coalitions could keep political authority, community trust, resources, and accountability aligned over time. Leadership in scale-up is therefore less about control and more about alignment of incentives, narratives, authority, and accountability.

This chapter focuses on three interrelated dimensions of that alignment. First, it examines how leaders identify and mobilize key players, paying particular attention to informal power and political endorsement. Second, it explores how political

DOI: 10.4324/9781003685821-13

and cultural landscapes shape scale-up trajectories, drawing on empirical examples such as Rwanda's national rollout of the Human Papillomavirus (HPV) vaccine and the Meningitis Vaccine Project (MVP) in Burkina Faso and across the African meningitis belt. Third, it analyzes negotiation and conflict management as core leadership practices, rather than as signs of failure. Throughout, the chapter emphasizes that stakeholder engagement is not a preparatory step to scale-up, but the work of scale itself. Together, the HPV vaccine rollout in Rwanda and the MVP illustrate contrasting but complementary models of coalition-building at scale, spanning nationally anchored political alignment and regionally coordinated, cross-border governance.

Scale is depicted as an ongoing condition sustained through alignment across four interdependent domains: political legitimacy and authority; cultural legitimacy and trust; resource alignment and capacity; and accountability, negotiation, and learning. Leadership is conceptualized as relational work that maintains coherence across these domains over time.

To clarify what "leadership as alignment" means in practice, Figure 9.1 presents a systems-level view of sustained scale-up. The central claim is simple: scale is not a one-time achievement but an ongoing condition. Leaders sustain scale by continually aligning political authority, cultural trust, resources, and accountability as contexts shift. These four domains are mutually reinforcing. Political legitimacy enables coordination and resource mobilization; cultural legitimacy determines uptake and compliance; resource alignment sustains delivery capacity;

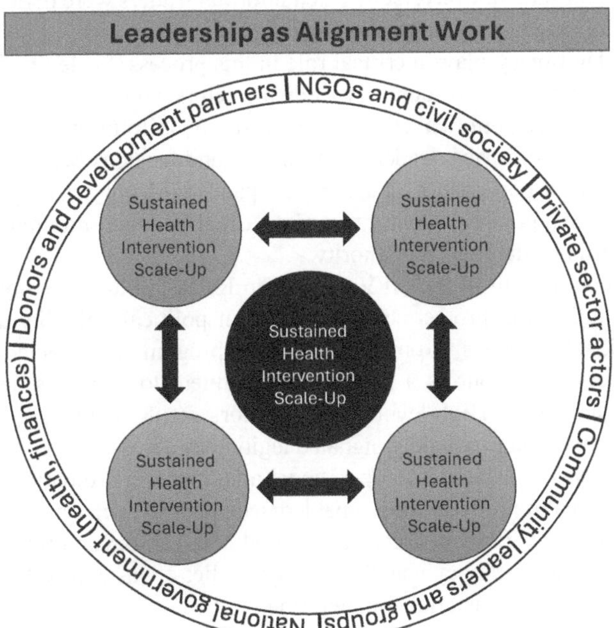

Figure 9.1 Leadership as Alignment Work in Sustaining Scale

and accountability and learning provide the feedback loops that allow coalitions to adapt. Scale erodes when any one domain drifts out of alignment, even if the intervention remains technically sound.

Identifying and Mobilizing Key Players

Coalitions do not form automatically around effective interventions. They are built deliberately, negotiated continuously, and sustained through leadership judgment. In practice, this means moving beyond stakeholder lists toward an ongoing assessment of who holds influence, how it is exercised, and when it shifts.

Stakeholders in health scale-up extend far beyond implementing organizations or ministries of health. They include political leaders, donors, frontline workers, professional associations, civil society organizations, private sector actors, and community representatives. Each brings distinct incentives, resources, and forms of influence. Across previously published interview-based studies, one pattern emerged consistently: formal authority rarely captures where real power lies.[5]

In many scale-up efforts documented in earlier research, individuals without senior titles shaped outcomes by controlling information flows, coordinating across fragmented institutions, or mediating between national policy and local implementation realities.[5] These actors often operated outside formal governance structures, yet their influence proved decisive. When stakeholder engagement focused narrowly on organizational charts and official mandates, coalitions weakened and implementation stalled. Conversely, when informal leaders were deliberately identified and mobilized, scale-up gained traction.

Political legitimacy plays a critical role in this process. Scale requires political endorsement to mobilize resources, coordinate actors, and sustain implementation over time.[6] However, political endorsement is rarely uniform or stable. Competing priorities across ministries, leadership turnover, and tensions between centralized and decentralized governance structures frequently disrupt scale-up trajectories. Leaders who treat political support as a given often find their programs vulnerable to sudden shifts in attention or authority.

The national rollout of the HPV vaccine in Rwanda illustrates how deliberate coalition-building can protect scale efforts from political volatility and competing institutional priorities. From the outset, the program was framed not only as a health intervention, but as a national commitment to women's health, cancer prevention, and equity. High-level political endorsement, including visible support from senior government officials, signaled legitimacy across sectors. Crucially, this endorsement was translated into operational alignment: coordination between the ministries of health and education enabled school-based delivery, while engagement with local government structures ensured outreach beyond formal schooling systems. Political legitimacy was thus not symbolic; it was embedded in routines, mandates, and inter-ministerial collaboration.

Mobilizing key players also required attention to cultural legitimacy and trust. In Rwanda, community health workers, teachers, and local leaders played central roles as intermediaries between national policy and household decision-making.[7]

Their involvement was not incidental. By leveraging trusted actors who understood local concerns and social norms, the coalition reduced uncertainty and resistance, enabling rapid uptake. This experience reinforces a broader lesson from scale-up across Africa: legitimacy flows not only from national authority, but from alignment with community values and lived realities.

A contrasting but complementary example comes from the MVP, which culminated in the development and rollout of MenAfriVac across the African meningitis belt, including Burkina Faso.[8] The success of MVP depended on a complex coalition involving international donors, scientific institutions, national governments, and regional bodies. While scientific leadership was essential, scale was ultimately achieved through political commitment at the country level and coordination across borders. Burkina Faso's early adoption of the vaccine demonstrated how national leadership, when aligned with regional priorities and global financing mechanisms, could accelerate scale while maintaining local ownership.[5]

In both cases, stakeholder mobilization was not a one-time event. As scale progressed, new actors entered the coalition, implementation challenges emerged, and narratives had to be revisited. Leadership involved maintaining alignment under changing conditions, rather than assuming that early consensus would endure.

Beyond HPV and MVP, effective stakeholder engagement in scale-up requires deliberate strategies tailored to different categories of actors, each with distinct sources of influence and incentives. National governments, particularly ministries of health and finance, play a foundational role in setting policy priorities, authorizing national scale, embedding interventions within public systems, and stabilizing long-term financing. Their influence derives from regulatory authority, control over public budgets, and stewardship over health systems. Across cases examined in earlier work, scale-up efforts that aligned early with national priorities and were formally adopted into policy frameworks and budgetary plans were far more likely to endure. Mexico's Seguro Popular provides a salient illustration: government stewardship converted a reform initiative into an institutionalized national scale by embedding it within law and public financing mechanisms, insulating it from political turnover.[6] Where national governments were bypassed or engaged late, donor-driven parallel systems emerged, weakening institutionalization and increasing the risk of policy reversal and sustainability failure.

International donors constitute another critical stakeholder group in scale-up. Donors can act as funders, capacity builders, intermediaries, and coordinators, and their control over financial resources and global networks enables them to shape government decisions.[9] Their incentives often include advancing thematic priorities, strengthening systems, and maintaining long-term partnerships. Effective engagement requires aligning scale-up plans with donor priorities while demonstrating effectiveness, scalability, and credible financial stewardship. When donors are engaged strategically, they can enable interventions to scale across multiple countries. When they are not, scale-up efforts risk fragmentation, fiscal instability, and weakened institutional ownership.

Non-governmental organizations (NGOs) and civil society actors often operate at the interface between systems and communities, providing direct services, advocating for change, and building local capacity. Their influence stems from social legitimacy and proximity to communities, which positions them as critical brokers in scale-up. Successful efforts have leveraged NGOs through training, social mobilization, and resource-sharing arrangements. A classic example is BRAC, a Bangladesh-based development organization, which scaled oral rehydration therapy nationally by training millions of mothers. This helped embed Oral Rehydration Therapy (ORT) use as a social norm and dramatically reduced child mortality from diarrheal disease.[10,11] When NGOs are inadequately engaged, scale-up efforts often suffer from weak beneficiary accountability and poor alignment with local needs.

Private sector actors represent an increasingly important but complex stakeholder group in scale-up. They can contribute financial resources, technical expertise, operational efficiency, and innovative business models that accelerate adoption. Incentives often include corporate responsibility, reputation, and market expansion. Public–private partnerships that co-design solutions with governments and civil society have enabled pilot initiatives to transition to scale. Excluding private actors can limit innovation, reduce solution diversity, and slow momentum.

Community leaders and groups play a critical role in translating scale-up efforts into locally legitimate action.[12] They contribute local knowledge, social practices, and trust, and often serve as intermediaries between communities and external actors. When community actors are engaged as coalition partners rather than end-users, scale-up efforts are more likely to adapt to local realities, sustain momentum, and reinforce legitimacy. When they are overlooked, trust erodes, opportunities for localization are missed, and long-term impact is diminished.

Together, these examples reinforce a core lesson: stakeholder identification and engagement must be differentiated, intentional, and iterative. Leadership in scale-up involves recognizing the distinct roles, incentives, and risks associated with each stakeholder category and aligning them with the long-term goals of the intervention.

Navigating Political and Cultural Landscapes

Once key actors are mobilized, leaders confront a second, often more complex task: navigating the political and cultural conditions that determine whether coalitions can endure. These conditions are rarely neutral. They are shaped by history, power, belief, and memory, and they can either stabilize scale or quietly undermine it.

Scaling health interventions requires leaders to engage not only with organizational stakeholders, but also with the political and cultural landscapes that shape whether scale is possible, legitimate, and durable. Political authority determines who can authorize action, mobilize resources, and coordinate across sectors. Cultural beliefs and norms influence whether communities accept, reinterpret, or resist interventions. Historical trust in institutions shapes compliance and cooperation, while power asymmetries determine whose priorities are privileged in decision-making. Across these scale-up efforts, these dimensions repeatedly emerged as decisive, often determining success or failure irrespective of technical merit.

Political Legitimacy and Authority

Political legitimacy is a foundational condition for scale. Without political endorsement, even highly effective interventions struggle to mobilize resources, coordinate actors, or sustain implementation over time.[6] Yet political legitimacy is rarely uniform across government. Competing priorities between ministries, leadership turnover, and tensions between centralized and decentralized systems can fragment authority and quietly stall scale-up.

Across the cases examined in this book, political will was rarely expressed through policy statements alone. Instead, it became visible through practical actions: which ministry chaired coordination meetings, how quickly regulatory or administrative barriers were resolved, and whether senior leaders were willing to publicly associate themselves with interventions facing resistance. Political endorsement functioned less as rhetoric than as a signal to the system, shaping behavior across bureaucratic levels and influencing how seriously scale-up efforts were taken by implementers and partners.

The national rollout of the HPV vaccine in Rwanda illustrates how political legitimacy can be deliberately constructed and sustained. From the outset, the program benefited from strong national endorsement, including visible commitment from senior political leaders. Importantly, this legitimacy was not symbolic. It was operationalized through formal inter-ministerial coordination, integration into national health and education plans, and alignment with Rwanda's broader development agenda centered on equity and human capital. By embedding the intervention within policy frameworks and routine systems, political legitimacy was insulated from leadership turnover and electoral cycles.

By contrast, scale-up efforts that rely primarily on individual champions without institutionalization remain vulnerable. Across multiple African contexts, programs stalled or were reversed following changes in political leadership when scale-up goals had not been embedded into law, budgets, or formal governance mechanisms. National health reforms in Mexico demonstrate the opposite dynamic: legal mandates and institutional design enabled reforms to persist beyond electoral cycles, stabilizing scale at the national level. Leadership, in this context, involved aligning scale-up goals with national political agendas and policy windows, transforming political support into durable institutional commitments.

Cultural Beliefs and Norms

Cultural beliefs and norms shape how interventions are interpreted, accepted, and sustained. Scale is not determined solely by technical effectiveness or delivery efficiency, but by whether interventions resonate with local values, histories, and social meanings. Religious interpretations, traditional health practices, and collective memory all influence whether communities embrace scale-up efforts or resist them.

Across vaccination programs, resistance was rarely rooted in ignorance or lack of information. More often, it reflected deeply held beliefs, historical experiences with external authority, and concerns about autonomy and control. When leaders treated resistance as a deficit of knowledge to be corrected, scale stalled. When they treated it as a signal to be understood, engagement strategies evolved and coalitions strengthened.

Resistance to polio vaccination in parts of Northern Nigeria illustrates the consequences of failing to engage cultural dynamics. In this context, local religious and cultural leaders framed the vaccine as unsafe and politically motivated, leading several states to refuse participation and significantly delaying eradication efforts.[13] Technical evidence alone proved insufficient to overcome this resistance. Progress occurred only when leadership strategies shifted toward engaging trusted local figures, adapting communication to local belief systems, and rebuilding a sense of community ownership over the intervention.

The Rwandan HPV experience highlights a contrasting approach. Anticipating concerns related to fertility, morality, and safety, program leaders invested early in culturally grounded messaging and engagement. Teachers, community health workers, and local leaders were equipped to address questions in ways that resonated locally, translating biomedical evidence into shared meaning rather than abstract assurance. This cultural fluency reduced uncertainty, normalized uptake, and reinforced trust, demonstrating that leadership in scale-up requires attention not only to what is delivered, but to how it is understood.

Ignoring cultural norms carries clear risks. Across contexts, failure to engage communities produced low uptake, mistrust, backlash, and stalled implementation. By contrast, interventions that treated culture as a determinant of scale, rather than as an implementation detail, were more likely to achieve sustained adoption. Leadership in this domain involved listening before persuading, engaging before correcting, and building legitimacy through shared meaning rather than authority alone.

Historical Trust in Institutions

Historical trust in public institutions shapes whether scale-up efforts are met with cooperation or resistance. Trust influences willingness to comply with guidance, accept collective action, and interpret government intent as protective rather than coercive. Where institutional trust is high, scale-up efforts benefit from a presumption of legitimacy. Where trust is low, even well-designed interventions encounter skepticism and delay.

Trust is not produced at the moment of crisis or scale-up. It reflects long-standing experiences with governance, including histories of inclusion or exclusion, corruption or accountability, and reliable or inconsistent service delivery. These accumulated experiences shape how communities interpret new interventions and whether they view them as credible or threatening.

The Ebola response in Liberia illustrates the consequences of low institutional trust. Years of conflict and weak public services had eroded confidence in state institutions, leading many communities to resist public health measures during the outbreak. This resistance slowed the scale-up of critical interventions, exacerbated transmission, and undermined response efforts.[14] The challenge was not simply technical capacity, but the absence of a trust foundation on which scale could be built.

Across contexts examined here, leadership strategies that emphasized transparency, inclusion, and responsiveness were essential to rebuilding trust over time. Engagement with communities, clear communication about uncertainty, and visible accountability for decisions helped shift perceptions of government intent and capability. Where historical distrust was ignored, social cohesion weakened, compliance declined, and the capacity to respond to complex challenges was severely constrained. Trust, in this sense, functioned not as a background condition, but as an active determinant of whether scale was possible.

Power Asymmetries

Power asymmetries shape whose priorities define interventions, who controls resources, and whose knowledge is valued in decision-making. In many scale-up efforts, authority is centralized while responsibility is decentralized, leaving local actors accountable for implementation without meaningful influence over strategy or resources. These dynamics often remain implicit, yet they profoundly shape scale outcomes.

Across these cases, power asymmetries frequently manifested as donor dominance, centralized planning, and the marginalization of district-level implementers. In such settings, local actors were expected to adapt interventions to complex realities without the authority or flexibility to do so. The result was often frustration, superficial compliance, and limited learning.

The PERFORM2Scale initiative illustrates how unresolved power imbalances can undermine scale-up. District managers were tasked with implementing health management strengthening interventions, yet national-level actors retained control over resources and strategic decisions. This imbalance slowed implementation, constrained local adaptation, and generated tension between system levels.[15] Scale advanced only when leadership responses explicitly addressed power by introducing shared decision-making structures, strengthening capacity at lower levels, and creating space for local problem-solving.

Where power asymmetries were ignored, scale-up became top-down, poorly owned, and inconsistently implemented. Where they were acknowledged and deliberately managed, scale became more adaptive and resilient. Leadership in these contexts required making power visible, redistributing authority in practical ways, and designing governance arrangements that supported learning rather than compliance alone.

As Figure 9.1 summarizes, sustained scale depends less on linear expansion than on keeping political authority, cultural trust, resources, and accountability aligned as conditions change.

Negotiation and Conflict Resolution in Scale-Up

As coalitions expand and resources are reallocated, tension becomes unavoidable. The question is not whether conflict will arise, but how leaders respond when it does. In scale-up, conflict is best understood not as breakdown, but as information, revealing where alignment is incomplete, incentives are misaligned, or assumptions no longer hold.

As health interventions move from pilot to scale, conflict becomes an expected feature of complex systems. Scale-up redistributes resources, redefines roles, and elevates certain priorities over others, creating friction among actors with differing incentives and values. Across the cases examined in this book, conflict repeatedly surfaced at moments when systems were under strain and coalitions required renegotiation.

Leadership in scale-up, therefore, requires treating negotiation and conflict resolution as core practices rather than peripheral skills. Effective leaders anticipated recurring sources of tension, recognized early signals of misalignment, and intervened in ways that preserved coalition integrity while enabling adaptation.

Resource Allocation Conflicts

As programs expand, competition over funding, staff, and infrastructure intensifies. Governments, donors, and implementing partners operate under constrained budgets and distinct accountability pressures, making disagreements over priorities inevitable. In many scale-up efforts, resource conflicts emerged precisely at the point when pilot funding gave way to questions of long-term financing and sustainability.

Health financing reforms illustrate how negotiated approaches to resource allocation can mitigate these tensions. Rwanda's Mutuelles de Santé required sustained negotiation among government agencies, donors, and communities to align financing mechanisms and ensure equitable coverage. Transparent priority-setting and explicit trade-offs were central to maintaining trust and preventing fragmentation as the program scaled nationally.[16] Where such negotiations were absent or opaque, coalitions fractured and scale became uneven.

Leadership in these contexts involved political negotiation and coalition management rather than technical optimization alone. Leaders who acknowledged constraints openly and involved stakeholders in priority-setting were better positioned to sustain alignment. By contrast, top-down allocation decisions eroded trust and reinforced perceptions of inequity, undermining coalition stability.

Role Ambiguity and Boundary Disputes

As interventions scale, roles and responsibilities often shift faster than formal governance arrangements can adjust. This creates ambiguity about authority, accountability, and expectations, particularly for frontline implementers operating across multiple systems. When roles are unclear, performance suffers, coordination weakens, and conflict becomes personalized rather than structural.

Across scale-up efforts, boundary disputes frequently emerged where professional hierarchies intersected or where new responsibilities were layered onto existing roles without clarification. Leadership responses that clarified expectations, standardized responsibilities across units, and reinforced regular feedback reduced friction and improved coordination. Boundary-setting proved especially critical in multi-sectoral initiatives, where overlapping mandates and norms increased the risk of confusion.

Where role ambiguity was left unaddressed, its effects cascaded across the system. Interprofessional conflict intensified, accountability weakened, and service quality declined. In scale-up contexts, these dysfunctions were magnified, as unclear roles at one level reverberated through interconnected institutions. Leadership in such settings required deliberate attention to role design, authority alignment, and the ongoing renegotiation of responsibilities as scale evolved.

Ideological Disagreement

Some conflicts in scale-up reflect ideological disagreement rather than technical dispute. Differences in values, moral commitments, and identities shape how stakeholders interpret evidence, risk, and policy choices. These conflicts are especially salient in interventions that intersect with personal autonomy, social norms, or deeply held beliefs, where evidence alone rarely resolves disagreement.

During the COVID-19 pandemic, mask-wearing became an ideological symbol. For some, it represented solidarity and collective responsibility; for others, it signaled government overreach and loss of autonomy.[17] Similar dynamics have emerged in vaccination campaigns and reproductive health interventions, where acceptance has been shaped less by information deficits than by identity, trust, and perceived legitimacy.

Across cases examined in this book, leadership in such contexts required ideological awareness rather than technical persuasion. Leaders who acknowledged underlying values, framed interventions in ways that resonated across perspectives, and created space for dialogue were more effective in sustaining coalitions. Where ideological conflict was ignored or dismissed as irrational, scale-up efforts stalled, trust eroded, and polarization intensified.

Accountability Disputes

Accountability disputes represent another recurrent source of tension in scale-up. As interventions expand, expectations around performance, reporting, and responsibility often become ambiguous. When success metrics are unclear or accountability is framed punitively, transparency declines and blame-shifting becomes more likely.

In multi-level scale-up efforts, ministries, funders, and local implementers frequently hold divergent assumptions about who is responsible for outcomes and how performance should be assessed. Where these assumptions remain implicit, accountability becomes contested rather than shared. Leadership responses that clarified expectations, defined success collaboratively, and modeled accountability through consistent follow-through strengthened trust and coordination.

Where accountability disputes were left unresolved, coalitions weakened. Implementers became defensive, problems went unreported, and learning stalled. In some cases, mistrust escalated to the withdrawal of funding or political support.

Across contexts, accountability proved most effective when it supported adaptation and learning rather than compliance alone.

Across these conflict types, a unifying lesson emerged: negotiation in scale-up is not a single event, but a continuous process. Leaders who treated conflict as diagnostic information rather than as failure were better positioned to recalibrate coalitions, realign incentives, and sustain momentum over time.

Leadership Moves

Leadership in stakeholder engagement and coalition-building is not about eliminating tension or achieving permanent consensus. It is about exercising disciplined judgment in systems shaped by power, history, and competing values, and sustaining that judgment as conditions evolve.

- **Map influence, not just formal authority.** Formal titles rarely capture who shapes outcomes in practice. Effective leaders identify informal power, understand who controls information and trust, and update these assessments as coalitions shift over time.
- **Anchor scale within institutional mandates early.** Political endorsement can accelerate expansion, but durability depends on embedding commitments in policy, budgets, and governance arrangements. Institutionalization protects scale from leadership turnover and electoral cycles.
- **Treat culture and trust as structural determinants.** Historical experience with institutions, social norms, and perceptions of legitimacy shape uptake as powerfully as technical evidence. Leaders must engage these dynamics deliberately rather than relegating them to communication strategy.
- **Anticipate conflict as a predictable feature of scale.** Resource competition, role ambiguity, ideological disagreement, and accountability disputes are inherent to coalition work. Addressed early and negotiated transparently, they can strengthen alignment; ignored, they fracture it.
- **Protect coalitions through transparency and follow-through.** Trust is reinforced when leaders acknowledge constraints, communicate decisions clearly, and deliver consistently. Sustained scale depends less on eliminating disagreement than on governing power and trust so that disagreement strengthens alignment rather than eroding it.

References

1. Atun R, de Jongh T, Secci F, Ohiri K, Adeyi O. Integration of targeted health interventions into health systems: a conceptual framework for analysis. Health Policy Plan. 2010 Mar 1;25(2):104–11.
2. Howitt P, Darzi A, Yang GZ, Ashrafian H, Atun R, Barlow J, et al. Technologies for global health. The Lancet. 2012 Aug 4;380(9840):507–35.
3. Bryson JM, Crosby BC, Stone MM. Designing and implementing cross-sector collaborations: needed and challenging. Public Adm Rev. 2015;75(5):647–63.

4. Ansell C, Gash A. Collaborative governance in theory and practice. J Public Adm Res Theory. 2008 Oct 1;18(4):543–71.
5. Ezezika O. Scaling up health innovations in Africa: prospects and challenges. Toronto: University of Toronto Press; 2025. 246 p.
6. Frenk J, González-Pier E, Gómez-Dantés O, Lezana MA, Knaul FM. Comprehensive reform to improve health system performance in Mexico. The Lancet. 2006 Oct 28; 368(9546):1524–34.
7. Ezezika O, Purwaha M, Patel H, Mengistu M. The Human Papillomavirus Vaccine Project in Rwanda: lessons for vaccine implementation effectiveness. Glob Implement Res Appl. 2022 Dec 1;2(4):394–403.
8. Ezezika O, Mengistu M, Lear T. Implementation of the Meningitis Vaccine Project in Africa: lessons for vaccine implementation programs. J Glob Health Rep [Internet]. 2021 Nov 2 [cited 2026 Feb 18];5. Available from: https://www.joghr.org/article/29042-implementation-of-the-meningitis-vaccine-project-in-africa-lessons-for-vaccine-implementation-programs
9. Biesma RG, Brugha R, Harmer A, Walsh A, Spicer N, Walt G. The effects of global health initiatives on country health systems: a review of the evidence from HIV/AIDS control. Health Policy Plan. 2009 Jul 1;24(4):239–52.
10. Cash RA. Using Oral Rehydration Therapy (ORT) in the community. Trop Med Infect Dis [Internet]. 2021 May 28 [cited 2026 Jan 30];6(2). Available from: https://www.mdpi.com/2414-6366/6/2/92
11. Chowdhury AMR, Karim F, Sarkar S, Cash RA, Bhuiya A. The status of ORT in Bangladesh: how widely is it used? Health Policy Plan. 1997 Jan 1;12(1):58–66.
12. Greenhalgh T, Robert G, Macfarlane F, Bate P, Kyriakidou O. Diffusion of innovations in service organizations: systematic review and recommendations. Milbank Q. 2004;82(4):581–629.
13. Yahya M. Polio vaccines – "no thank you!" barriers to polio eradication in northern Nigeria [Internet]. Rochester, NY: Social Science Research Network; 2009 [cited 2026 Jan 30]. Available from: https://papers.ssrn.com/abstract=1436304
14. Blair RA, Morse BS, Tsai LL. Public health and public trust: survey evidence from the Ebola Virus Disease epidemic in Liberia. Soc Sci Med. 2017 Jan 1;172:89–97.
15. Raven J, Mansour W, Aikins M, Bulthuis S, Chikaphupha K, Dieleman M, et al. From PERFORM to PERFORM2Scale: lessons from scaling-up a health management strengthening intervention to support Universal Health Coverage in three African countries. Health Policy Plan. 2024 Sep 10;39(8):841–53.
16. Lu C, Chin B, Lewandowski JL, Basinga P, Hirschhorn LR, Hill K, et al. Towards universal health coverage: an evaluation of Rwanda Mutuelles in its first eight years. PloS One. 2012;7(6):e39282.
17. Young DG, Bleakley A. Ideological health spirals: an integrated political and health communication approach to COVID interventions. Int J Commun. 2020 Jun 7;14:17–17.

10 Financing and Resource Mobilization for Scale

Scaling health interventions is ultimately a question of financing, but not in the narrow sense of whether money exists. It is a question of how resources are mobilized, through which institutions, under what political assumptions, and with what expectations about time, accountability, and public obligation. Across global health experience, the pattern is consistent. Many interventions that demonstrate strong effectiveness at the pilot stage falter at scale not because the intervention stops working, but because the financing model collapses under the weight of expanded ambition.

This chapter advances a central claim. Financing decisions are among the most consequential leadership choices in scale-up. They determine whether scale becomes a durable public commitment or a fragile, projectized expansion. They shape who bears costs, who benefits, and who is held accountable when trade-offs emerge. Financing is therefore not merely a technical enabler of scale. It is a political and institutional architecture that actively structures scale trajectories.

What makes financing for scale especially difficult is that it embeds assumptions about the role of the state, the market, and external actors. Every financing model implies a theory of governance. It implies who should pay, when they should pay, and what happens when resources fall short. It implies how risk is distributed and whose needs take priority when fiscal constraints tighten. Leaders rarely articulate these assumptions explicitly, yet they become visible as soon as scale accelerates and systems are tested. In this sense, financing for scale is the design of obligations over time.

This chapter focuses on three interrelated dimensions of financing for scale. First, it examines blended financing approaches that combine public, private, and philanthropic resources, highlighting both their catalytic potential and their structural risks. Second, it analyzes sustainable funding models, emphasizing how different arrangements enable some forms of scale while undermining others. Third, it interrogates cost-effectiveness and return on investment arguments, showing how economic evidence is mobilized politically.

Throughout, the emphasis is on leadership judgment. Financing models do not fail or succeed on their own. They are stabilized or destabilized by decisions leaders make when utilization rises faster than capacity, when political commitments outrun fiscal space, and when short-term gains threaten long-term viability.

DOI: 10.4324/9781003685821-14

Table 10.1 Financing Choices and Consequences for Scale

Financing approach	*What it enables early*	*What emerges as obligations expand*	*Leadership risk*	*What stabilizes scale*
1. Short-term project or pilot funding	Rapid launch; proof of concept	Funding cliff; service interruption	Treating pilots as precursors to sustainability	Early transition planning into routine public budgets
2. Donor-led vertical financing	Fast coverage expansion; visible gains	Fragmentation; dependency; parallel systems	Substituting donor funds for long-term system investment	Integration into national budgeting, payroll, and procurement systems
3. Blended financing without public absorption plan	Accelerated rollout; rapid political momentum	Cost overruns; unclear ownership; fiscal stress	Diffuse accountability and delayed transition planning	Clear fiscal transition pathways and state stewardship
4. Market-only/ out-of-pocket financing	Speed; consumer choice; minimal public coordination	Inequitable access; volatile demand; legitimacy erosion	Mistaking uptake for population coverage	Strategic public purchasing, subsidies, and regulatory oversight
5. Insurance-based pooling	Risk sharing; financial protection	Political and administrative strain at high coverage; exclusion of informal populations	Assuming voluntarism will achieve universality	Subsidization, mandatory enrollment, and pool unification
6. Tax-funded public financing	Equity; universality; predictable public entitlement	Vulnerability during fiscal downturns and competing budget pressures	Political backlash over sustained health spending	Cross-sector fiscal commitment and continuous political defense of health budgets

Table 10.1 shows how financing decisions shape the trajectory of scale over time, distinguishing between rapid but fragile expansion and slower pathways that ultimately produce sustained, system-embedded coverage.

Governing Blended Financing for Durable Scale

Blended financing has become one of the defining features of contemporary global health scale-up. Governments draw on public budgets while engaging donors, philanthropies, and increasingly private actors to fund ambitious initiatives. These arrangements are often presented as pragmatic responses to constrained fiscal space. In many cases, they have enabled rapid expansion of coverage that would not have been possible through domestic financing alone.

Yet blended financing is not a neutral technical solution. It is a negotiated political settlement among actors with different time horizons, accountability standards, and definitions of success. Donors may prioritize measurable results within funding cycles. Philanthropies may seek innovation and demonstrable impact. Governments must manage long-term obligations, public expectations, and fiscal sustainability. When these logics are misaligned, blended financing can accelerate scale in the short term while embedding fragility in the system.

The central leadership challenge in blended financing is therefore not assembling resources, but aligning obligations. External funds can accelerate scale, but only leadership decisions determine whether they become a bridge to durable public financing or a substitute that delays difficult choices.

Early Financing Choices and Path Dependency

Early financing decisions shape scale trajectories in ways that are difficult to reverse. Many initiatives begin with pilot grants, time-limited donor funding, or exceptional budget lines that sit outside routine public financing. The implicit assumption is that sustainability can be addressed later, once success has been demonstrated. Table 10.1 categorizes common early financing approaches and the leadership risks they create as scale expands.

In practice, later arrives quickly. Utilization increases. Political attention intensifies. The true operating costs of scale become visible. At this point, financing models that were adequate for pilots often prove insufficient for national delivery.

Mexico's Seguro Popular illustrates how leadership can convert early blended financing into durable institutional architecture. The reform sought national universal health coverage and initially relied on public budgets complemented by transition financing. As donor resources proved time-limited and questions arose about long-term fiscal sustainability, political leadership acted decisively. Financing was institutionalized through legislation, with earmarked public funds and formal budgetary commitments involving national and subnational governments. This move transformed Seguro Popular from a reform initiative into a public entitlement anchored in law and fiscal governance. Scale was stabilized not because resources increased dramatically overnight, but because financing obligations were made explicit, enforceable, and politically protected.[1]

Uganda's abolition of user fees demonstrates the risks when early financing decisions do not anticipate scale effects. The removal of fees was a powerful political commitment to equity, financed through reallocated and increased government budgets. Utilization rose sharply, particularly among poorer populations. At the same time, facilities lost a key revenue source, and drug shortages and quality concerns emerged as demand outpaced supply-side financing. Leadership responded with short-term injections of funds for drugs and health worker wages, including substantial salary increases, and introduced private paying wings in hospitals to cross-subsidize services. While access improved, recurring budget shortfalls persisted, producing a pattern of high utilization alongside constrained quality.[2]

This contrast reveals a core leadership lesson. Blended financing and reform momentum can deliver rapid access gains, but unless early decisions account for how scale changes cost structures and expectations, systems become locked into cycles of reactive financing rather than planned sustainability.

Blended Financing as Acceleration

Blended financing is most effective when it is explicitly designed as acceleration capital. In such cases, external resources are used to expand fiscal space temporarily while domestic institutions build capacity to absorb recurrent costs.

This requires deliberate choices. External funds must support system functions rather than bypass them. They must finance supply chains, workforce expansion, supervision, and information systems alongside commodities and services. Most importantly, they must be linked to a credible transition pathway that specifies which costs will be absorbed domestically, by whom, and on what timeline.

Ghana's National Health Insurance Scheme illustrates both the promise and the limits of blended financing used for acceleration. Launched with the ambition of achieving universal health coverage within five years, the scheme relied on an earmarked health insurance levy combined with member premiums and external support. Early gains were substantial, with rapid enrollment and increased service use. However, benefit packages and exemptions expanded faster than contributions, and informal sector enrollment lagged. The insurance fund became strained, leading to recurring deficits within a few years.[3]

Government responses included increasing the levy, subsidizing premiums for the poor, and introducing cost control measures. These adjustments stabilized the scheme temporarily but did not resolve the underlying tension between political ambition and fiscal capacity. The experience demonstrates that blended financing can accelerate access, but without continuous recalibration and disciplined benefit design, it can also institutionalize fiscal stress.

Rwanda's experience with national health insurance reflects a more tightly governed use of blended financing. Community-based insurance schemes were supported through member premiums alongside government and external subsidies for the poorest. When voluntary enrollment limited coverage and fragmented pools strained administrative capacity, leadership intervened. Insurance membership was made mandatory, pools were unified nationally, and subsidies were institutionalized through public financing. External resources supported this transition rather than substituting for it. The result was high coverage, reduced out-of-pocket spending, and sustained utilization gains, albeit with ongoing reliance on government financing to subsidize premiums.[4,5]

The lesson is not that blended financing eliminates sustainability challenges. Rather, it shows that blended financing can be disciplined by strong state stewardship that treats external funds as instruments for building durable public systems.

Blended Financing and Dependency Risks

The most persistent risk of blended financing is dependency. When external resources finance core operating costs without a transition plan, systems can achieve impressive short-term gains while becoming structurally vulnerable.

Sierra Leone's Free Health Care Initiative provides a vivid illustration. Launched as a presidential initiative to provide free care for pregnant women, mothers, and children under 5, the program relied on government leadership paired with substantial external financing for drugs and health worker salaries. Salary increases were mandated to eliminate informal fees, and partners supported supply chains, audits, and monitoring. Utilization increased immediately, with large gains in facility deliveries and child health visits. At the same time, the share of external financing in national health spending rose sharply, raising concerns about long-term dependency and the sustainability of recurrent costs.[6,7]

This case highlights a recurring leadership dilemma. Blended financing can save lives quickly, but without a clear pathway to domestic absorption, it creates a financing cliff. Leaders must then confront politically costly decisions about scaling back benefits, increasing domestic revenue, or renegotiating external commitments.

The broader lesson is that blended financing should be judged not only by the amount of money it mobilizes, but by what it finances and what it leaves behind. If external resources finance parallel systems or substitute for public responsibility, scale remains fragile. If they finance capacity, institutions, and transition, they can underpin durable scale.

Sustainable Funding Models

Sustainable funding is often framed as the search for the right model. In practice, sustainability emerges from alignment. Financing mechanisms must align with administrative capacity, political norms, and social expectations. Each model enables certain forms of scale while constraining others. Different funding models distribute those obligations in different ways; leadership lies in recognizing these trade-offs and adapting financing arrangements as scale evolves.

Pooled Insurance and Solidarity

Pooled social and community-based insurance schemes are often promoted as equity-oriented mechanisms for financing scale. By spreading risk across populations, they can provide predictable funding and reduce out-of-pocket spending. However, they depend heavily on administrative capacity, social trust, and political enforcement. Pooled insurance offers predictability and equity, but only when backed by enforcement, subsidies, and sustained political commitment.

Rwanda's national insurance system demonstrates how leadership can strengthen pooled financing through governance. Mandatory enrollment, national pooling, and sustained subsidies were not technical tweaks. They were political decisions that prioritized solidarity over voluntarism. The result was high coverage and reduced financial barriers, achieved through continuous fiscal commitment and administrative investment.[4,5]

By contrast, where pooled insurance remains fragmented or voluntary, coverage often stalls among informal and poor populations. Without enforcement and subsidies, pooled models risk reproducing inequities rather than resolving them.

Tax-Funded National Systems

General tax-funded systems represent a different theory of scale. They treat health care as a public entitlement financed through general revenues. Thailand's Universal Coverage Scheme illustrates the strengths of this model. Broad risk pooling and tax financing dramatically reduced out-of-pocket spending and expanded access. At the same time, the model relies on sustained political commitment to protect health budgets during economic fluctuations and competing fiscal priorities.[8] Tax-funded systems promote equity and universality, but their durability depends on continuous political defense during fiscal downturns.

The sustainability of tax-funded systems depends less on technical design than on political leadership. Leaders must continuously defend health spending as a public good rather than a discretionary expense. When political commitment weakens, quality and coverage erode.

Mandatory Social Health Insurance

Payroll-based social health insurance offers a dedicated funding stream that is less vulnerable to annual budget negotiations. It can rapidly expand coverage among formal sector workers. However, it often excludes informal populations unless explicitly subsidized, creating two-tier systems.

Ghana's experience illustrates this tension. While the insurance scheme expanded access, sustaining generous benefits required repeated fiscal interventions. Without subsidies and strong administrative capacity, mandatory insurance risks becoming regressive or fiscally unstable.[3,9]

Demand-Side Financing

Demand-side financing mechanisms such as conditional cash transfers aim to stimulate utilization by reducing financial barriers for households. They have been effective in increasing the use of priority services, particularly maternal and child health services. Demand-side incentives can rapidly increase utilization, but without parallel supply-side investment they expose quality and capacity constraints.

India's Janani Suraksha Yojana and Nepal's Aama Safe Delivery Program show how incentives can rapidly shift behavior. Institutional deliveries increased substantially. However, these gains exposed supply-side constraints. Facilities became overcrowded, reimbursement delays created friction, and quality risks emerged. Leadership responses included phased expansion, increased budget allocations, and investments in workforce and infrastructure.[10,11]

These cases underscore a fundamental point. Incentives can pull demand, but sustainable scale requires financing the system that meets that demand.

Donor-Funded Vertical Programs

Donor-funded vertical programs represent another influential funding model in global health scale-up. These programs have delivered some of the fastest and most visible health gains in recent decades, particularly in HIV, immunization, malaria, and tuberculosis. By concentrating resources on specific diseases or interventions, they have enabled rapid expansion of coverage in settings where domestic financing alone would have been insufficient.

At the same time, vertical financing introduces well-documented sustainability challenges. Because funds are often earmarked for specific activities, they can bypass national budgeting processes, create parallel delivery systems, and distort workforce incentives. When external funding wanes or eligibility thresholds are crossed, countries face abrupt transitions that expose gaps in domestic financing and system integration. Experiences from countries graduating from immunization support have shown that maintaining coverage requires early planning for domestic absorption of vaccine procurement, cold-chain maintenance, and service delivery costs.[12,13]

The leadership challenge in vertical financing is therefore not whether to accept donor funds, but how to integrate them. Programs that are treated as exceptional or temporary often struggle to survive beyond the funding cycle. Programs that are deliberately embedded into national financing frameworks, with clear plans for absorbing recurrent costs, are more likely to endure. This requires leaders to resist the temptation to pursue short-term performance gains at the expense of long-term system coherence.

Out-of-Pocket Financing

Out-of-pocket financing through user fees remains one of the most contested funding models in global health. Historically justified as a way to generate facility-level revenue and improve service availability, user fees have repeatedly been shown to undermine equity and deter utilization among the poorest populations. Evidence from the Bamako Initiative era demonstrated that while fees could temporarily improve drug availability, they imposed substantial financial barriers and social costs, leading many countries to reverse or modify fee-based systems.[2,14,15]

From a leadership perspective, user fees illustrate a broader lesson about sustainable scale. Financing mechanisms that rely on excluding those least able to pay may stabilize budgets in the short term, but they erode legitimacy and undermine the very objectives of scale. Sustainable funding models must align with social values and political commitments to equity, not merely with fiscal convenience.

Across these models, a consistent pattern emerges. Sustainability is not inherent in any single financing arrangement. It is produced through continuous alignment between financing mechanisms, delivery capacity, political expectations, and social norms. Leaders must anticipate that scale changes the system they are financing. Models that work at low coverage often behave very differently at high coverage. Sustainable scale requires leaders who are willing to revisit financing choices, recalibrate benefits, and renegotiate obligations as conditions evolve.

Cost-Effectiveness and Return on Investment Arguments

Economic arguments play a central role in decisions about scale. Cost-effectiveness analyses, return on investment estimates, and macroeconomic projections are widely used to justify investments in health interventions. These tools provide a common language for engaging ministries of finance, donors, and political leaders who must allocate scarce resources across competing priorities.

Yet economic evidence does not operate in a vacuum. It is mobilized strategically, framed selectively, and interpreted through political lenses. Understanding how cost-effectiveness and return on investment arguments function in practice is essential for leaders seeking to scale health interventions sustainably.

Global disease prioritization initiatives have long relied on cost per disability-adjusted life year averted as a benchmark for allocating resources.[16] This approach has helped direct funding toward interventions that deliver large health gains per dollar spent. However, it has also privileged interventions that are easy to measure and model, sometimes at the expense of investments in system capacity and long-term sustainability. Programs funded primarily on the basis of cost-effectiveness can achieve impressive short-term results while remaining fragile if delivery systems are underfinanced.

National immunization programs provide a clear illustration of the power and limits of return on investment arguments. Vaccination has been framed as one of the highest-return investments in health, with analyses showing substantial future savings to health systems and economies for every dollar spent.[17] These arguments have been instrumental in mobilizing global and domestic resources and expanding coverage. At the same time, return on investment calculations often aggregate benefits across populations, obscuring distributional issues and the political challenge of transitioning to domestic financing once external support declines.[12] Leaders who rely solely on return on investment narratives may find themselves unprepared for the fiscal and political work required to sustain coverage.

Family planning initiatives illustrate another dimension of economic justification. Framed in terms of cost savings through prevention, particularly avoided costs associated with unintended pregnancies and maternal complications, family planning has gained traction with budget officials and donors.[18] While these arguments have been effective in mobilizing resources, they risk narrowing the policy discourse. By emphasizing savings, they can understate the broader social benefits of reproductive autonomy, gender equity, and empowerment. Leaders must therefore balance economic reasoning with normative commitments if scale is to be both politically legitimate and socially grounded.

Non-communicable disease (NCD) prevention has increasingly been framed as a macroeconomic investment, with "best buys" promising substantial returns in terms of productivity gains and reduced future health costs.[19] This framing has elevated NCDs on national and global agendas, particularly among finance ministries and development banks. However, implementation has often lagged behind rhetoric. Industry opposition, regulatory complexity, and short electoral cycles have slowed the adoption of policies such as tobacco taxation and marketing restrictions. These cases demonstrate a recurring limitation of economic arguments. Strong economic logic does not automatically translate into political action. Leaders must be prepared to confront vested interests and invest political capital to realize the promised returns.

Mental health interventions provide a more optimistic example of economic evidence enabling scale. The Friendship Bench program demonstrated that task-shifted psychotherapy delivered by lay workers could achieve meaningful improvements in mental health outcomes at relatively low cost.[20] Economic analyses strengthened the case for scale and contributed to national adoption and international replication.[21] Yet even here, leadership mattered. Scaling required financing supervision, training, and quality assurance, costs that are not always fully captured in early economic models. Without attention to these elements, cost-effective interventions risk losing fidelity as they expand.

HIV prevention and education-linked interventions further illustrate the political nature of economic justification. Voluntary medical male circumcision has been promoted as a cost-saving intervention that reduces future treatment costs by preventing new infections.[22,23] Large-scale donor-backed programs achieved rapid expansion in multiple countries. Over time, however, coverage plateaued as social acceptability challenges and funding fatigue emerged. Similarly, school-based deworming programs have been justified through high return on investment narratives emphasizing long-term gains in education and income.[24,25] These arguments unlocked multisectoral support, but they also raised concerns about overgeneralization and the need for complementary investments in sanitation and reinfection control.

Across these cases, a consistent lesson emerges. Cost-effectiveness and return on investment arguments are powerful tools for opening doors. They help interventions compete for attention and resources. They are rarely sufficient to sustain scale. Economic evidence answers the question of whether an intervention is worth funding. It does not answer the harder questions of who will pay repeatedly, how quality will be protected as coverage expands, and how systems will adapt when conditions change.

Leaders who rely exclusively on economic arguments risk mistaking persuasion for implementation. Sustainable scale requires translating economic value into financing pathways that assign ownership, distribute risk, and embed accountability over time.

In my experience, the most fragile scale-ups are not those that lack evidence, but those where leaders mistake persuasive economic arguments for a financing strategy. Economic value does not assign responsibility; financing architecture does.

Leadership Moves

Financing for scale is the design of obligations over time. Durable scale depends less on how much money is mobilized than on how responsibility, risk, and accountability are structured as coverage expands.

- **Design financing architecture early.** Treat funding sources, pooling arrangements, and transition pathways as foundational design decisions. Early choices shape political expectations and become difficult to reverse once utilization rises.
- **Use blended financing as acceleration capital, not substitution.** External resources should temporarily expand fiscal space while domestic institutions build capacity to absorb recurrent costs. Without a defined transition pathway, acceleration becomes dependency.
- **Anticipate the second-order costs of success.** Rapid increases in utilization expose hidden expenditures in workforce, supervision, supply chains, administration, and quality assurance. Plan for these costs before fiscal strain destabilizes reform.
- **Integrate external funding into national systems.** Parallel financing may deliver speed, but durable scale requires embedding programs into routine budgeting, payroll, procurement, and accountability structures with clear domestic ownership.
- **Balance ambition with fiscal realism.** Calibrate expansion commitments to administrative capacity, revenue trajectories, and the recurrent costs created by rising utilization. Political promises should be matched by financing pathways that can survive beyond launch.
- **Protect quality and equity as obligations grow.** Use disciplined benefit design, verification, supervision, and performance safeguards to prevent volume incentives from degrading care or widening inequities. Scale endures when financing protects both access and quality.

References

1. Frenk J, González-Pier E, Gómez-Dantés O, Lezana MA, Knaul FM. Comprehensive reform to improve health system performance in Mexico. The Lancet. 2006 Oct 28;368(9546):1524–34.
2. Nabyonga Orem J, Mugisha F, Kirunga C, Macq J, Criel B. Abolition of user fees: the Uganda paradox. Health Policy Plan. 2011 Sep 1;26(suppl_2):ii41–51.
3. Alhassan RK, Nketiah-Amponsah E, Arhinful DK. A review of the National Health Insurance scheme in Ghana: what are the sustainability threats and prospects? PLOS ONE. 2016 Nov 10;11(11):e0165151.
4. Lu C, Chin B, Lewandowski JL, Basinga P, Hirschhorn LR, Hill K, et al. Towards universal health coverage: an evaluation of Rwanda Mutuelles in its first eight years. PLOS ONE. 2012 Jun 18;7(6):e39282.
5. Chemouni B. The political path to universal health coverage: power, ideas and community-based health insurance in Rwanda. World Development. 2018 Jun 1;106:87–98.

6. Spry E. Emily Spry: the free health care initiative in Sierra Leone [Internet]. The BMJ. 2010 [cited 2026 Jan 31]. Available from: https://blogs.bmj.com/bmj/2010/04/22/emily-spry-the-free-health-care-initiative-in-sierra-leone/
7. Witter S, Wurie H, Bertone MP. The Free Health Care Initiative (FHCI) in Sierra Leone: real gains for mothers and young children [Internet]. UK Department for International Development.; 2016 [cited 2026 Jan 31] p. 4. Available from: https://assets.publishing.service.gov.uk/media/585a9c8f40f0b60e4c0000f7/The-Free-Health-Care-Initiative-in-Sierra-Leone-real-gains-for-mothers-and-young-children.pdf
8. Tangcharoensathien V, Witthayapipopsakul W, Panichkriangkrai W, Patcharanarumol W, Mills A. Health systems development in Thailand: a solid platform for successful implementation of universal health coverage. The Lancet. 2018 Mar 24;391(10126):1205–23.
9. Le QN, Blizzard L, Si L, Giang LT, Neil AL. The evolution of social health insurance in Vietnam and its role towards achieving universal health coverage. Health Policy OPEN. 2020 Dec 1;1:100011.
10. Gupta SK, Pal DK, Tiwari R, Garg R, Shrivastava AK, Sarawagi R, et al. Impact of Janani Suraksha Yojana on institutional delivery rate and maternal morbidity and mortality: an observational study in India. Journal of Health, Population and Nutrition. 2012;30(4):464–71.
11. Ensor T, Bhatt H, Tiwari S. Incentivizing universal safe delivery in Nepal: 10 years of experience. Health Policy Plan. 2017 Oct 1;32(8):1185–92.
12. Saxenian H, Hecht R, Kaddar M, Schmitt S, Ryckman T, Cornejo S. Overcoming challenges to sustainable immunization financing: early experiences from GAVI graduating countries. Health Policy Plan. 2015 Mar 1;30(2):197–205.
13. Kolesar RJ, Spruk R, Tsheten T. Evaluating country performance after transitioning from Gavi assistance: an applied synthetic control analysis [Internet]. Global Health: Science and Practice. 2023 Aug 28 [cited 2026 Jan 31];11(4). Available from: https://www.ghspjournal.org/content/11/4/e2200536
14. Knippenberg R, Nafo FT, Osseni R, Camara YB, Abassi AE, Soucat A. Increasing clients' power to scale up health services for the poor: THE BAMAKO INITIATIVE IN WEST AFRICA Background paper to the World Development Report. 2003 Jul;34.
15. Uzochukwu BS, Onwujekwe OE, Akpala CO. Effect of the Bamako-Initiative drug revolving fund on availability and rational use of essential drugs in primary health care facilities in south-east Nigeria. Health Policy Plan. 2002 Dec 1;17(4):378–83.
16. Murray CJL, Lopez AD. Measuring the global burden of disease. New England Journal of Medicine. 2013 Aug 1;369(5):448–57.
17. Johns Hopkins Bloomberg School of Public Health. Expanding use of vaccines could save up to $44 for every dollar spent, study suggests [Internet]. 2016 [cited 2026 Jan 31]. Available from: https://publichealth.jhu.edu/2016/expanding-use-of-vaccines-could-save-up-to-44-dollars-for-every-dollar-spent-study-suggests
18. Guttmacher. Guttmacher releases most comprehensive evidence to date on global family planning gaps, investment and economic returns [Internet]. 2025 [cited 2026 Jan 31]. Available from: https://www.guttmacher.org/news-release/2025/guttmacher-releases-most-comprehensive-evidence-date-global-family-planning-gaps
19. World Health Organization. WHO urges cost effective solutions on NCDs and mental health amidst slowing progress [Internet]. 2025 [cited 2026 Jan 31]. Available from: https://www.who.int/news/item/18-09-2025-who-urges-cost-effective-solutions-on-ncds-and-mental-health-amidst-slowing-progress

20. Chibanda D, Weiss HA, Verhey R, Simms V, Munjoma R, Rusakaniko S, et al. Effect of a primary care-based psychological intervention on symptoms of common mental disorders in Zimbabwe: a randomized clinical trial. JAMA. 2016 Dec 27;316(24):2618–26.
21. Healey A, Verhey R, Mosweu I, Boadu J, Chibanda D, Chitiyo C, et al. Economic threshold analysis of delivering a task-sharing treatment for common mental disorders at scale: the Friendship Bench, Zimbabwe. Evid Based Mental Health [Internet]. 2022 Apr 21 [cited 2026 Jan 31];25(2). Available from: https://mentalhealth.bmj.com/content/25/2/47
22. Njeuhmeli E, Forsythe S, Reed J, Opuni M, Bollinger L, Heard N, et al. Voluntary medical male circumcision: modeling the impact and cost of expanding male circumcision for HIV prevention in Eastern and Southern Africa. PLOS Medicine. 2011 Nov 29;8(11):e1001132.
23. World Health Organization. Voluntary medical male circumcision [Internet]. 2023 [cited 2026 Jan 31]. Available from: https://www.who.int/teams/global-hiv-hepatitis-and-stis-programmes/hiv/prevention/voluntary-medical-male-circumcision
24. Miguel E, Kremer M. Worms: Identifying impacts on education and health in the presence of treatment externalities. Econometrica. 2004;72(1):159–217.
25. Abdul Latif Jameel Poverty Action Lab (J-PAL). Deworming to increase school attendance [Internet]. 2022 [cited 2026 Jan 31]. Available from: https://www.povertyactionlab.org/case-study/deworming-increase-school-attendance

11 Innovation, Adaptation, and Continuous Learning

Why Scale Requires Learning, Not Replication

Innovation in global health is often described as a breakthrough moment: a new vaccine, a promising technology, or an intervention shown to work under controlled conditions. Yet experience across health systems shows that the most consequential work begins after innovation. Evidence alone rarely translates into durable population-level impact. What determines whether innovations endure is not only the strength of their evidence base, but whether leaders design systems capable of learning as interventions move from pilots to scale.

Across low-, middle-, and high-income settings alike, interventions encounter cultural norms, political incentives, workforce constraints, and resource limitations that were not fully anticipated at the design stage. When programs stall or collapse, the cause is rarely scientific failure. More often, it reflects a failure to govern adaptation. Interventions are rolled out as if scale were a technical exercise in replication rather than a dynamic process requiring structured feedback, disciplined modification, and continuous recalibration.

Implementation science provides leaders with concepts and tools for navigating this challenge. It clarifies what must remain stable, what can change responsibly, and how learning should guide decision-making over time. This chapter examines how leaders preserve core mechanisms while allowing delivery forms to evolve, how feedback loops are institutionalized, and how data become infrastructure for improvement rather than compliance. The argument is direct: scale is not sustained through replication of form, but through disciplined learning that protects purpose while enabling adaptation.

Implementation Science as Organized Learning

Implementation science emerged in response to a persistent gap between evidence and practice. While clinical and public health research excels at establishing efficacy, it has historically paid less attention to how interventions are adopted, implemented, and sustained in real-world systems. Implementation science shifts attention from whether an intervention works to how it works in context, for whom, and under what conditions.

DOI: 10.4324/9781003685821-15

A defining contribution of implementation science is its emphasis on context. Contemporary frameworks highlight the multiple levels that shape implementation, including organizational culture, leadership engagement, external policy environments, and frontline workflows. These frameworks are not recipes for success. Rather, they are tools for diagnosing barriers, guiding adaptation, and supporting learning over time.

One of the most practically useful insights from implementation science is the distinction between core functions and forms. Core functions refer to the mechanisms through which an intervention produces its effects. Forms refer to the specific ways those mechanisms are delivered in practice. When scale-up efforts conflate the two, implementation becomes rigid and fragile. Programs are judged by whether they look the same everywhere, rather than by whether they achieve the same underlying purpose.

Implementation science reframes adaptation not as deviation from fidelity, but as a condition for effectiveness at scale. Protecting core mechanisms while allowing delivery strategies to adapt enables interventions to remain effective across diverse settings.

Adaptation Across Contexts: Lessons From Practice

The following cases show how learning enables scale across leadership challenges such as legitimacy, reliability, system fit, workforce design, and sustained behavior change.

Surgical Safety and the Politics of Legitimacy

The World Health Organization's Surgical Safety Checklist illustrates how adaptation and learning shape successful scale-up. Developed as a standardized perioperative tool, the checklist was shown to reduce morbidity and mortality across diverse hospital settings.[1,2] Its global diffusion, however, revealed substantial variation in uptake.

In district hospitals with hierarchical clinical cultures and staffing constraints, the checklist was sometimes perceived as an externally imposed requirement. Resistance from senior clinicians limited use, and time pressures undermined adherence. Feedback from audits and staff interviews revealed that opposition was directed less at the goal of safety than at the way the checklist was introduced.

By distinguishing core safety functions from delivery form, leaders were able to adapt implementation without undermining intent. Local champions reframed the checklist as a communication and teamwork tool. Roles were clarified, language was adapted, and ownership shifted toward local teams. Over time, adherence improved and safety gains were sustained. This case demonstrates that legitimacy is built through adaptation informed by systematic feedback.

Reliability Through Continuous Learning in Infection Prevention

Central-line-associated bloodstream infection (CLABSI) prevention provides a complementary example of learning-driven implementation. Evidence-based bundles outlining best practices for line insertion and maintenance are well established, yet inconsistent adherence often limits their impact.

In an adult coronary intensive care unit with persistently high infection rates, leaders embedded learning into daily practice. Using Plan–Do–Study–Act cycles guided by the Model for Improvement, teams preserved core bundle elements while introducing real-time audits, simulation training, and daily compliance checks.[3]

Surveillance data and run charts enabled teams to observe trends, test adjustments, and refine practices. Infections were eliminated for a sustained period, not through a single change but through continuous learning. This case illustrates how reliability emerges when feedback loops are institutionalized rather than episodic.

Safe Childbirth and Sustaining Attention Over Time

The WHO Safe Childbirth Checklist was designed to ensure completion of essential birth practices during facility-based deliveries. Despite strong evidence, early implementation revealed low adoption, incomplete use, and declining attention after initial rollout.

Implementation strategies such as training, local champions, supervision, and audit and feedback were used to support adaptation.[4] Core practices were preserved, while translation, alignment with national guidelines, and formatting changes improved fit with local workflows.

Sustained adoption followed not because the checklist was redesigned, but because learning mechanisms were embedded into routine practice. Leadership engagement reinforced accountability while allowing contextual adaptation. This case highlights the importance of sustaining attention over time for interventions competing with multiple clinical priorities.

Differentiated Service Delivery and Learning at Scale in HIV Care

HIV differentiated service delivery (DSD) offers one of the clearest examples of adaptation becoming institutionalized at scale. As antiretroviral therapy programs expanded globally, many countries initially relied on highly standardized, facility-based delivery models designed to ensure clinical oversight and accountability. These models were effective in early expansion phases, when rapid initiation and tight monitoring were paramount. Over time, however, they became increasingly misaligned with the realities of long-term HIV care.

Routine program data and facility-level experience revealed a growing mismatch between service design and patient need. Clinically stable patients were required to attend frequent facility visits despite limited marginal benefit, while clinics became congested and health workers overextended. These pressures were visible in appointment backlogs, waiting times, and retention patterns, signaling the need for adaptation.

DSD emerged through structured learning rather than a single policy shift. Leaders preserved the core function of HIV programs—sustained viral suppression and retention in care—while adapting delivery forms to better align with patient needs and system capacity. Differentiated models included multi-month dispensing of antiretroviral therapy, fast-track refills, community adherence groups, and decentralized community-based distribution. Evidence consistently demonstrated that these adaptations reduced facility burden and improved patient experience while maintaining clinical outcomes.[5,6]

Crucially, differentiation was legitimized through national policy rather than treated as an exception. Guidelines evolved to permit variation in visit frequency, location of care, and cadre of provider based on patient stability. Monitoring systems continued to track viral suppression and retention, allowing leaders to assess whether adapted models preserved effectiveness or not. Where outcomes weakened, delivery strategies were refined, reinforcing the role of feedback in guiding adaptation.

DSD illustrates how continuous learning can be embedded into large-scale programs. Adaptation was framed not as a loss of fidelity, but as responsible stewardship of both clinical outcomes and system capacity. Leadership mattered less in prescribing a single model than in authorizing flexibility, trusting data from practice, and allowing evidence to reshape service delivery over time.

Building Local Capacity for Mental Health Scale-Up

Experiences from large-scale primary health care reforms illustrate how workforce models evolve through learning rather than remaining fixed. Ethiopia's Health Extension Program and Brazil's Family Health Strategy provide contrasting but complementary examples of how leaders institutionalized adaptation at national scale.

In Ethiopia, the Health Extension Program extended essential services to rural and underserved communities through salaried community-based health workers.[7,8] Over time, delivery models evolved in response to supervision data, community uptake, and performance monitoring. Task portfolios were adjusted, training curricula refined, and referral relationships strengthened as leaders learned what combinations of skills, incentives, and supervision were required to sustain performance at scale. Rather than remaining static, the program matured through iterative learning embedded within routine management.

Brazil's Family Health Strategy similarly demonstrates adaptation through decentralized learning.[9,10] Multidisciplinary teams anchored in defined geographic catchment areas adapted service delivery to local epidemiological and social conditions, supported by municipal governance and performance monitoring. Variation across municipalities was not treated as failure but as a source of learning, allowing effective practices to diffuse through policy and financing mechanisms.

Together, these cases reinforce a core lesson: workforce-based interventions scale when leaders treat delivery models as evolving systems rather than static designs.

The Kigali Imbereheza Project demonstrates how this leadership logic applies in mental health scale-up. In urban public HIV clinics with limited specialist capacity, trauma-informed cognitive behavioral therapy was adapted for delivery by trained youth leaders living with HIV.[11] Using the EPIS (Exploration, Preparation, Implementation, and Sustainment) framework, leaders preserved core therapeutic principles while authorizing task shifting, cultural tailoring, and ongoing supervision. Stakeholder engagement, fidelity assessments, and participant feedback created continuous learning loops that guided refinement over time.

The result was high acceptability, strong fidelity, and sustained delivery capacity. This case underscores that mental health interventions scale not through rigid adherence to specialist models, but through leadership that invests in local capacity and treats implementation as a learning process rather than a fixed protocol.

Treating National Programs as Learning Systems

The evolution of the directly observed treatment strategy for tuberculosis illustrates adaptation at system scale. Initially designed as a highly standardized, facility-based approach, rigid application exposed limitations in decentralized health systems, including access barriers and implementation burden.

By treating scale-up as a learning process, leaders preserved core treatment mechanisms while adapting delivery toward more community-based and patient-centered models. In practice, this meant authorizing flexibility in where and by whom treatment was supervised, strengthening links between health facilities and community actors, and using surveillance data and program evaluations to refine delivery strategies over time. These adjustments allowed programs to evolve in response to local realities without compromising treatment effectiveness.[12]

This case demonstrates that large-scale programs endure not by remaining unchanged, but by institutionalizing learning and allowing delivery models to evolve in response to evidence from practice.

Handwashing and Hygiene: Learning Beyond Awareness

Handwashing is often described as one of the simplest and most cost-effective public health interventions. Its biological effectiveness is uncontested, and its relevance spans infectious disease prevention, maternal and newborn health, and outbreak control. Yet despite decades of promotion, sustained handwashing with water and soap remains uneven, particularly in low-resource settings. This gap reflects a familiar challenge in scale-up: effectiveness does not translate into impact without attention to behavior, systems, and learning. Early hand hygiene efforts assumed awareness would drive behavior change, yet practice remained low even where knowledge was high.

Large-scale handwashing initiatives show how learning reshapes implementation over time. Programs that achieved durable gains moved beyond messaging to address infrastructure, incentives, and feedback together. In health facilities, the WHO Multimodal Hand Hygiene Improvement Strategy combined system change, training, monitoring, reminders, and leadership engagement. When implementation was treated as adaptive work, monitoring of compliance and consumption data enabled teams to identify bottlenecks, test adjustments, and refine delivery, supporting sustained improvement.[13]

Table 11.1 Leadership Patterns in Adaptation and Continuous Learning at Scale

Intervention	*Core Adaptation*	*Learning Trigger*	*Leadership Lesson (Key Evidence)*
1. WHO Surgical Safety Checklist	Delivery adapted, safety core preserved	Audit data, staff feedback	Protect core mechanisms while localizing delivery (Haynes et al., 2009; Weiser et al., 2010)[1,2]
2. CLABSI Prevention Bundle	Feedback embedded into daily practice	Surveillance data, run charts	Reliability improves when learning is continuous (Gupta et al., 2021)[3]
3. WHO Safe Childbirth Checklist	Format and ownership adapted	Audit and feedback	Accountability sustains fidelity when aligned to context (Gama et al., 2025)[4]
4. HIV Differentiated Service Delivery	Delivery differentiated by patient stability	Program monitoring and patient outcomes	Institutionalize adaptation through policy (Grimsrud et al., 2016; WHO, 2016)[5,6]
5. Kigali Imbereheza Project	Task-shifted delivery model	Fidelity and stakeholder feedback	Invest in local capacity to sustain scale (Donenberg et al., 2019)[11]
6. DOTS Tuberculosis Strategy	Community-centered delivery	Program evaluation data	Treat scale-up as a learning process (Raviglione & Uplekar, 2006)[12]
7. WHO Hand Hygiene Strategy	Infrastructure adapted locally	Compliance monitoring	Sustained change requires leadership commitment (Pfäfflin et al., 2017)[13]

These experiences align with broader implementation evidence. A multi-country systematic review shows that hand hygiene interventions are most effective when infrastructure, social reinforcement, and feedback mechanisms are addressed together rather than relying on education alone.[14] Sustained practice depends on how well interventions are adapted to local constraints and incorporated into routine workflows through ongoing learning.

Taken together, these cases reveal a consistent pattern. Interventions that achieve durable scale do so not by replicating delivery models, but by institutionalizing learning and adaptation over time. Table 11.1 distills these cross-cutting patterns, highlighting how leaders used feedback, policy, and system design to preserve core functions while adapting delivery across diverse contexts.

Learning Loops as Leadership Infrastructure

Across successful scale-up efforts, learning does not occur by accident. It is deliberately engineered by leaders through infrastructure that embeds feedback, reflection, and authority to act into routine practice. Data alone do not produce learning. Learning emerges when systems are designed to interpret evidence, test adjustments, and respond in real time.

Effective learning loops operate across multiple time horizons. Short-cycle feedback supports rapid course correction during implementation, while longer-term data inform strategic decisions about sustainability, resourcing, and institutionalization. When learning is confined to early pilots or external evaluations, systems struggle to adapt as scale introduces new constraints and trade-offs.

Leadership is therefore central to whether learning becomes episodic or durable. Leaders determine whether feedback mechanisms are resourced, whether teams are authorized to act on what data reveal, and whether adaptation is treated as responsible stewardship rather than failure. When learning loops are institutionalized, scale becomes a managed process of continuous improvement rather than a one-time expansion.

Leadership Moves

Leadership for scale requires governing learning deliberately. Innovation endures not because it is replicated faithfully, but because leaders design systems that adapt without losing purpose.

- **Specify and protect core mechanisms.** Leaders must distinguish between the causal mechanisms that generate impact and the delivery forms through which those mechanisms are expressed. Core functions should remain stable across contexts, while implementation strategies evolve. When this distinction is unclear, adaptation is mistaken for dilution and fidelity becomes rigid imitation rather than protection of purpose.
- **Embed learning within routine governance.** Feedback, reflection, and course correction must be built into everyday management rather than confined to pilots or external evaluations. Learning becomes durable only when monitoring systems, review processes, and authorized experimentation are normalized within institutional practice.
- **Signal that adaptation is legitimate and expected.** Adaptation should be framed as responsible stewardship under changing conditions, not as deviation from standards. Through endorsement, supervision, and resource allocation, leaders communicate that thoughtful modification is supported when it protects outcomes.
- **Build system capacity to interpret and act.** Sustainable scale depends on workforce capability to analyze performance, diagnose gaps, and adjust practice. Training and supervision are not peripheral investments; they are prerequisites for systems that can learn without constant external direction.
- **Use data as infrastructure for collective improvement.** Performance information should function as a shared resource for problem-solving rather than primarily as an instrument of compliance. When data are used for learning, reliability and equity strengthen; when used mainly for inspection, learning contracts.
- **Protect outcomes while permitting delivery variation.** Clear commitments to safety, effectiveness, and equity must coexist with contextual flexibility. Leaders hold firm on what must be achieved while allowing local strategies to evolve in response to constraint. Scale endures when adaptation is disciplined, learning is institutionalized, and purpose remains protected across changing conditions.

References

1. Haynes AB, Weiser TG, Berry WR, Lipsitz SR, Breizat AHS, Dellinger EP, et al. A surgical safety checklist to reduce morbidity and mortality in a global population. N Engl J Med. 2009 Jan 29;360(5):491–9.
2. Weiser TG, Haynes AB, Lashoher A, Dziekan G, Boorman DJ, Berry WR, et al. Perspectives in quality: designing the WHO Surgical Safety Checklist. Int J Qual Health Care. 2010 Oct 1;22(5):365–70.
3. Gupta P, Thomas M, Patel A, George R, Mathews L, Alex S, et al. Bundle approach used to achieve zero central line-associated bloodstream infections in an adult coronary intensive care unit. BMJ Open Qual [Internet]. 2021 Feb 17 [cited 2026 Feb 3];10(1). Available from: https://bmjopenquality.bmj.com/content/10/1/e001200
4. Gama ZA da S, Semrau KEA, Rosendo TMS de S, Freitas MR de, Saraiva COP de O, Westgard CM, et al. Implementation strategies for the WHO Safe Childbirth Checklist: a scoping review. BMJ Open. 2025 Dec 1;15(12):e112114.
5. Grimsrud A, Bygrave H, Doherty M, Ehrenkranz P, Ellman T, Ferris R, et al. Reimagining HIV service delivery: the role of differentiated care from prevention to suppression. J Int AIDS Soc. 2016;19(1):21484.
6. Global HIV, Hepatitis and STIs Programmes (HHS), Guidelines Review Committee. Consolidated guidelines on HIV prevention, diagnosis, treatment and care for key populations [Internet]. World Health Organization; 2016 Jul [cited 2026 Feb 3] p. 155. Available from: https://www.who.int/publications/i/item/9789241511124
7. Assefa Y, Hill PS, Gilks CF, Admassu M, Tesfaye D, Van Damme W. Primary health care contributions to universal health coverage, Ethiopia. Bull World Health Organ. 2020 Dec 1;98(12):894–905A.
8. Banteyerga H. Ethiopia's health extension program: improving health through community involvement. MEDICC Rev. 2011 Jul;13(3):46–9.
9. Paim J, Travassos C, Almeida C, Bahia L, Macinko J. The Brazilian health system: history, advances, and challenges. The Lancet. 2011 May 21;377(9779):1778–97.
10. Macinko J, Harris MJ. Brazil's family health strategy — delivering community-based primary care in a universal health system. N Engl J Med. 2015 Jun 4;372(23):2177–81.
11. Donenberg GR, Cohen MH, Ingabire C, Fabri M, Emerson E, Kendall AD, et al. Applying the Exploration Preparation Implementation Sustainment (EPIS) framework to the Kigali Imbereheza Project for Rwandan adolescents living with HIV. J Acquir Immune Defic Syndr. 2019 Dec;82 Suppl 3(Suppl 3):S289–98.
12. Raviglione MC, Uplekar MW. WHO's new Stop TB Strategy. The Lancet. 2006 Mar 18;367(9514):952–5.
13. Pfäfflin F, Tufa TB, Getachew M, Nigussie T, Schönfeld A, Häussinger D, et al. Implementation of the WHO multimodal Hand Hygiene Improvement Strategy in a University Hospital in Central Ethiopia. Antimicrob Resist Infect Control. 2017;6:3.
14. Ezezika O, Heng J, Fatima K, Mohamed A, Barrett K. What are the barriers and facilitators to community handwashing with water and soap? A systematic review. PLOS Glob Public Health. 2023 Apr 19;3(4):e0001720.

Part IV

The Discipline of Leadership

The earlier parts of this book established scale as a leadership problem unfolding across systems, institutions, and coalitions. They showed how authority fragments, incentives diverge, and uncertainty persists as initiatives move from controlled pilots into complex systems. Leaders must align institutions that do not share the same mandates, sustain cooperation among actors who retain autonomy, and adapt strategy as conditions evolve.

Part IV turns from the practice of scaling to the discipline of leadership that makes scale possible. If large-scale change unfolds under persistent uncertainty and distributed authority, then leadership cannot be understood solely as vision or personal capability. It requires a structured discipline: the capacity to make decisions under constraint, to govern systems that cannot be commanded, and to cultivate the institutional pathways through which such leadership is reproduced.

This section examines three interrelated dimensions of that discipline.

The first concerns judgment under constraint. As interventions expand, information remains incomplete, trade-offs intensify, and consequences extend across institutions and populations. Leadership therefore depends on the capacity to decide when evidence is sufficient to act, to redesign systems when strain appears, and to remain accountable for outcomes that cannot be fully controlled.

The second concerns governing distributed power. Large-scale health initiatives operate within polycentric systems in which authority is dispersed across governments, multilateral organizations, donors, private firms, and communities. No single actor commands the system. Leaders must therefore coordinate action through influence rather than hierarchy, stabilizing coalitions and aligning incentives among actors whose participation remains voluntary.

The third concerns leadership reproduction. If governing scale requires judgment and institutional fluency, the question becomes how such leaders emerge. Leadership capacity is not produced automatically by technical expertise. It is shaped by the institutional ecosystems that select, credential, and authorize who is recognized as legitimate within global health.

Together, these chapters argue that leadership at scale is not improvisation. It is a disciplined practice shaped by reasoning under uncertainty, governance across distributed authority, and institutional design that prepares future leaders to navigate complex systems.

DOI: 10.4324/9781003685821-16

12 Judgment at Scale

The Discipline of Decision Under Constraint

Throughout this book, scale has not been treated as expansion alone, but as a condition of constraint in which uncertainty persists, authority fragments, trade-offs intensify, and consequences reverberate across systems and over time. The cases examined show that strong evidence, adequate financing, and political endorsement do not eliminate complexity. Programs that are technically sound can stall, and reforms designed in good faith can produce unintended strain. At scale, the central challenge is not implementation alone; it is judgment.

Scale resists certainty. Information is incomplete, authority is distributed, and outcomes cannot be predicted with precision. Evidence informs action but rarely settles disagreement, and planning structures effort but cannot prevent disruption. In these conditions, leadership is defined not by control or confidence but by how leaders allocate uncertainty, redistribute complexity, and remain answerable for consequences they cannot fully control.

This chapter argues that sustained impact therefore depends on a distinctive leadership mindset: disciplined reasoning under uncertainty, adaptive redesign in the face of disruption, and ethical clarity amid unavoidable trade-offs. The focus shifts from what leaders did to how they thought. The aim is not to introduce new tools but to illuminate the cognitive discipline that allows leaders to act without illusion, adapt without losing direction, and accept moral residue without surrendering responsibility. Figure 12.1 summarizes this architecture of judgment and previews the three domains developed here.

This figure positions disciplined judgment under constraint as the central function of leadership at scale. The triangular structure integrates three domains: strategic allocation of uncertainty and risk, resilient redesign of systems under strain, and ethical governance of trade-offs and legitimacy. It argues that sustainable scale is not achieved by eliminating complexity or denying moral burden, but by allocating them consciously and transparently.

Strategic Thinking and Decision-Making Under Uncertainty

Scale punishes leaders who mistake strategy for certainty. Across the cases in this book, strategic leadership did not hinge on identifying an objectively optimal solution. It rested on deciding what counted as "good enough to act" when information

DOI: 10.4324/9781003685821-17

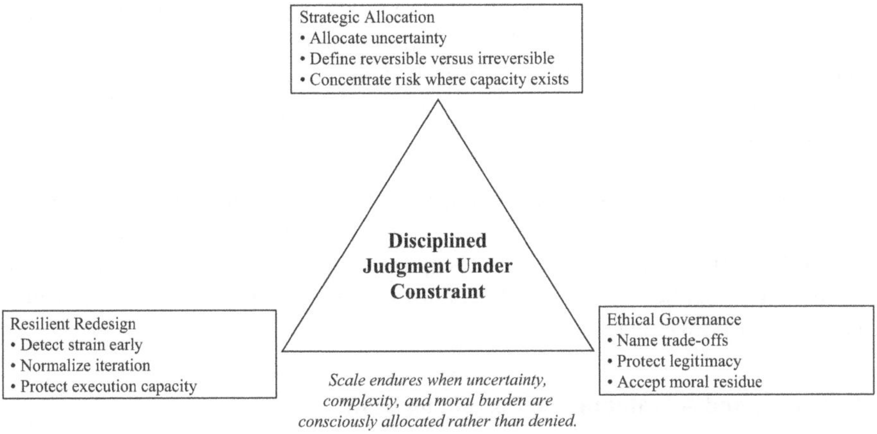

Figure 12.1 The Architecture of Judgment at Scale

was incomplete, authority was fragmented, and consequences were unevenly distributed. Strategy at scale is not the elimination of uncertainty; it is the disciplined choice of which uncertainties can be lived with and which risks require immediate action.[1,2]

A recurring pattern is that leaders often had to abandon familiar metrics and conventional sequencing. In smallpox eradication, the major strategic inflection point was not a new vaccine but a redefinition of success. Leaders shifted from mass vaccination targets to surveillance and containment, reframing the scale problem as interrupting transmission rather than maximizing coverage.[3,4] This was not simply a "technical adaptation." It was a leadership judgment that acknowledged unreliable surveillance data, uneven implementation reach, and the reality that universal coverage targets could paralyze action in thin systems where compliance could not be commanded. It was judgment under persistent informational uncertainty, acting where evidence was actionable rather than waiting for comprehensive certainty.[5]

MenAfriVac illustrates a different but related form of strategic judgment. Leaders faced a fundamental design question: should fragile systems be expected to meet the intervention's orthodox requirements, or should the intervention be redesigned to fit system constraints as they existed? The strategic answer favored feasibility over purity. Choices such as ultra-low price, single-dose formulation, thermostability, and the authorization pathway for controlled temperature chain delivery were strategic trade-offs under constraint, not merely technical features.[6,7] These decisions redistributed complexity—absorbing analytical and regulatory burdens upstream while simplifying execution downstream so overstretched systems could deliver protection.[6,7,8]

COVID-19 vaccine scale-up made the same strategic logic visible at unprecedented speed. Leaders could not preserve the conventional sequence of evidence, authorization, manufacturing, and delivery without accepting catastrophic delay. The governance decision was to overlap processes and redefine readiness as managed risk rather than evidentiary closure.[9] This created a lasting strategic tension between speed, equity, and legitimacy, intensified by evolving evidence and politicization. Leadership here involved the ability to govern iteration in public, rather than presenting shifting guidance as inconsistency or failure.[10]

Across these cases, leaders did not eliminate uncertainty; they allocated it deliberately. They simplified execution in weak systems, concentrated complex risk management where capacity was stronger, and treated strategy as a living discipline rather than a fixed plan.[11,12] Strategic thinking at scale is therefore not the search for optimal solutions, but the disciplined allocation of risk: deciding which uncertainties can be lived with, which must be mitigated immediately, and which can be deferred without illusion.

Resilience and Adaptability in Sustaining Scale

Resilience at scale is not persistence; it is redesign under strain. It is the capacity to continue making consequential decisions after disruption and to adjust systems before erosion becomes visible. Where scale endures, it does so because leaders treat breakdown as a governance signal rather than an episodic setback.

The malaria bed net case illustrates this vividly by reframing scale as a condition that must be continuously defended. Scientific uncertainty was not the barrier—nets were well established as reducing morbidity and mortality. The leadership challenge was durability under strain: protection eroded as nets tore, insecticide efficacy declined, use patterns shifted, and replacement systems repeatedly lagged behind need.[13,14] The near-failure was structural, not episodic. Coverage could appear impressive at distribution yet deteriorate as scale extended. Leaders who sustained progress treated breakdown as a governance signal rather than a setback. They shifted focus from one-time coverage to replenishment cycles, mixed delivery channels, and behavior-aligned strategies that recognized "authority without command" at the household level.

The Health Extension Program case adds the institutional dimension of resilience. Ethiopia's achievement was not simply deploying a cadre; it was institutionalizing a workforce and governance model capable of carrying primary care into rural settings without waiting for physician density to change.[15,16] As the program expanded, the leadership challenge evolved. Scale produced success, and success introduced overload risk. Resilience became the ability to shift from scale-up to stewardship, protecting the workforce contract through supervision, scope discipline, and reform rather than simply adding tasks to an already stretched platform.[17,18] This makes resilience concrete; it looks like system redesign and task governance, not inspirational persistence.

COVID-19 vaccine rollout shows resilience under political and social pressure. Adaptation was unavoidable: prioritization criteria, delivery models, and messaging had to shift as supply, variants, and evidence changed. Trust was not created by messaging alone; it was generated through governance. When revision was framed as inherent to crisis management and accountability remained clear, adaptation protected legitimacy. When revision appeared politically opportunistic or incoherent, uptake eroded despite vaccine availability.

Taken together, these cases support a crisp claim: resilience at scale is the ability to redesign after disruption without surrendering purpose or legitimacy. It is the habit of treating shocks as governance problems rather than reputational threats. This is the mindset leaders need if scale is to survive its own long tail.[12]

Ethical Considerations in Leadership for Scale

Ethics at scale is not primarily about avoiding harm. It is about governing trade-offs when harm cannot be eliminated and when benefits and burdens are distributed unevenly. This is why ethical leadership at scale produces moral residue: leaders can make defensible decisions and still carry the knowledge that someone bore costs that could not be fairly shared.

MenAfriVac provides a strong case for ethics as trade-offs rather than safeguards. The ethical dilemma was not limited to trial consent; it centered on whether it was legitimate to depart from regulatory orthodoxy in contexts marked by historical mistrust, including the shadow of the Pfizer Trovan controversy in Nigeria.[19] The controlled temperature chain decision was ethically fraught because cold-chain compliance operated as a moral standard as much as a technical one. Deviating from it risked being interpreted as lowering standards for African populations. Ethical leadership therefore required not only evidence but institutional protection and transparency. Global bodies and partners had to absorb reputational and regulatory risk so frontline workers and national managers were not left exposed. This is ethics as governance, not ethics as compliance.

COVID-19 made moral residue visible on a global scale. Allocation debates pitted national accountability against global equity. Booster decisions in high-income countries had direct implications for global supply and perceived fairness. Mandate debates exposed the tension between collective protection and autonomy, while politicization turned technical uncertainty into contested legitimacy. The leadership challenge was governing speed without eroding legitimacy and coordinating across borders without enforcement power. Ethical leadership required naming trade-offs openly and remaining accountable under contestation.

Smallpox eradication adds a deeper ethical layer. The campaign revealed a persistent tension between speed and legitimacy. Aggressive containment could trigger concealment, resistance, and stigma, especially where public authority was mistrusted.[20,21] The ethical dilemma was not only what to do, but how to do it without undermining the trust that surveillance and response depended upon. That is why decentralizing operational authority and privileging context-sensitive engagement were not just pragmatic choices. They were ethically necessary for compliance and legitimacy.

Ethical leadership at scale means choosing among imperfect options while remaining answerable for their consequences. Moral residue is not failure; it is the cost of governing systems where trade-offs are real and unavoidable.

Judgment as the Allocation of Risk and Responsibility

Across these cases, uncertainty, adaptation, and ethics converge in moments of judgment. Strategy forces leaders to decide what constitutes actionable readiness despite incomplete information. Resilience forces them to redesign systems after disruption without abandoning purpose. Ethics forces them to justify trade-offs when legitimacy is contested and when costs are externalized.

Across these examples, the recurring leadership act was a disciplined redistribution of risk and responsibility. Leaders simplified execution where systems were thin, shifted complexity upward to institutions capable of absorbing it, and governed adaptation without sacrificing legitimacy. Whether interrupting transmission in smallpox, redesigning vaccine delivery in MenAfriVac, institutionalizing task shifting in Ethiopia, sustaining malaria protection over time, or iterating COVID-19 vaccine rollout publicly, the underlying judgment was the same: scale endures when uncertainty, complexity, and moral burden are consciously allocated rather than denied.

Governing Legitimacy as an Operational Asset

Legitimacy is often treated as a reputational concern, but at scale, it is structural. It functions like infrastructure: when legitimacy weakens, information flows degrade, compliance becomes fragile, and implementation costs rise. Leaders who mistake legitimacy for communication rather than governance eventually discover that scale cannot be forced into existence.

At scale, authority disperses. Frontline workers interpret policy. Households reinterpret recommendations. Local officials filter guidance through political realities. Legitimacy determines whether these decentralized actors align with strategic intent or quietly resist it. It shapes whether data are reported accurately, interventions are used as intended, and policy revisions are interpreted as responsiveness or inconsistency.

Three properties of legitimacy become especially visible at scale. Legitimacy is cumulative, built over time through consistent alignment between promises and lived experience. It is asymmetric, far easier to lose than to restore. It is also contextual, meaning that it does not transfer automatically across communities, institutions, or crises.

Leaders at scale must therefore govern legitimacy deliberately by framing uncertainty transparently rather than concealing it, anticipating how rapid adaptation will be interpreted politically and socially, embedding accountability visibly within institutions, and avoiding strategies that achieve short-term technical gain at the expense of long-term trust.

Legitimacy is not a byproduct of scale; it is a precondition for it. When legitimacy collapses, technical systems falter, surveillance degrades, and uptake declines regardless of intervention quality.

The leadership mindset required here is simple but demanding: treat legitimacy as an operational variable that must be monitored, protected, and replenished just as deliberately as financing or supply chains.

Choosing Where Complexity Should Live

Complex systems do not simplify as they scale; they become more interconnected. The leadership challenge is not to eliminate complexity but to decide where it should reside.

Every scaled intervention generates complexity across multiple domains: logistics, financing, coordination, regulation, behavior, data systems, and political oversight. If complexity accumulates at the point of delivery, frontline actors become overwhelmed. If complexity is denied entirely, fragility emerges upstream.

Effective leaders redistribute complexity intentionally. They absorb coordination burdens at levels of the system that possess analytic and institutional capacity, while simplifying execution where capacity is thin. They design interventions that match the absorptive capacity of the environments in which they will operate.

This principle has three implications:

1. **Execution must be simpler than design.**
   Frontline implementation cannot carry the full burden of upstream policy complexity.
2. **Upstream actors must absorb uncertainty.**
   Regulatory bodies, global partners, and central institutions must manage ambiguity so peripheral actors are not immobilized by it.
3. **Complexity must be visible somewhere.**
   Simplification at one level always shifts burden elsewhere. Leaders must consciously choose where that burden falls.

When leaders fail to manage this redistribution, systems either stall under overload or collapse under hidden fragility. Sustainable scale emerges when complexity is allocated to the levels of the system best equipped to manage it without undermining legitimacy or performance.

The mindset shift is critical: scale is not simplification, but disciplined complexity management. Judgment at scale is not the elimination of uncertainty; it is the allocation of risk, complexity, and moral burden within systems that cannot be fully controlled.

Leadership Moves

These moves translate the chapter's argument into practical leadership disciplines for acting under uncertainty, protecting systems under strain, and remaining accountable for the trade-offs that scale makes unavoidable.

- **Treat certainty as provisional and decisions as iterative.** Plans provide direction, not permanence. Leaders act without waiting for complete information and assume revision is inevitable. Strategy defines orientation, not prediction. Delay in the pursuit of certainty can compound risk more than imperfect action.
- **Distinguish reversibility before accelerating action.** Speed is applied selectively. Reversible decisions create space for learning and can proceed quickly.

Irreversible commitments require structural caution and broader consultation. This distinction allows momentum without inviting systemic fragility.

- **Redistribute complexity to protect execution.** Scale does not eliminate complexity; it reallocates it. Frontline implementation must remain simpler than design. Analytical, regulatory, and coordination burdens should sit where institutional capacity can absorb them. When complexity accumulates at delivery points, performance erodes and legitimacy weakens.
- **Design systems that surface strain before collapse.** Fragility rarely announces itself. Leaders institutionalize feedback mechanisms that expose weak signals early and normalize adaptation as part of governance. Correction becomes routine rather than reactive.
- **Govern legitimacy as infrastructure.** Legitimacy enables compliance, coordination, and adaptation. It erodes faster than it accumulates and cannot be restored through messaging alone. Leaders protect credibility during revision and treat trust as an operational variable that must be monitored and replenished.
- **Name trade-offs and accept moral residue.** Scale redistributes benefit and burden unevenly. Even defensible decisions may impose unequal cost. Ethical discipline requires acknowledging trade-offs openly and remaining answerable for consequences that cannot be fully reconciled.

References

1. Mangham LJ, Hanson K. Scaling up in international health: what are the key issues? Health Policy Plan. 2010 Mar;25(2):85–96.
2. Yamey G. Scaling up global health interventions: a proposed framework for success. PLoS Med. 2011 Jun 28;8(6):e1001049.
3. Fenner F, Henderson DA, Arita I, Jezek Z, Ladnyi ID. Smallpox and its eradication. Geneva, Switzerland: World Health Organization; 1988.
4. Henderson DA. Smallpox — the death of a disease. J Clin Invest. 2009 Oct 1;119(10):2866.
5. Henderson DA. The eradication of smallpox. Sci Am. 1976 Oct;235(4):25–33.
6. PATH. The Meningitis Vaccine Project: a groundbreaking partnership [Internet]. 2015 [cited 2026 Feb 16]. Available from: https://www.path.org/our-impact/articles/about-meningitis-vaccine-project/
7. Zipursky S, Djingarey MH, Lodjo JC, Olodo L, Tiendrebeogo S, Ronveaux O. Benefits of using vaccines out of the cold chain: delivering meningitis A vaccine in a controlled temperature chain during the mass immunization campaign in Benin. Vaccine. 2014 Mar 14;32(13):1431–5.
8. Ezezika O, Mengistu M, Lear T. Implementation of the Meningitis Vaccine Project in Africa: lessons for vaccine implementation programs. J Glob Health Rep [Internet]. 2021 Nov 2 [cited 2026 Feb 16];5. Available from: https://www.joghr.org/article/29042-implementation-of-the-meningitis-vaccine-project-in-africa-lessons-for-vaccine-implementation-programs
9. Van Norman GA. "Warp speed" operations in the COVID-19 pandemic: moving too quickly? JACC Basic Transl Sci. 2020 Jul;5(7):730–4.
10. Moon S, Alonso Ruiz A, Vieira M. Averting future vaccine injustice. N Engl J Med. 2021 Jul 15;385(3):193–6.

11. Bradley EH, Curry LA, Taylor LA, Pallas SW, Talbert-Slagle K, Yuan C, et al. A model for scale up of family health innovations in low-income and middle-income settings: a mixed methods study. BMJ Open. 2012;2(4):e000987.
12. Peters DH, Adam T, Alonge O, Agyepong IA, Tran N. Implementation research: what it is and how to do it. BMJ. 2013 Nov 20;347:f6753.
13. Bhatt S, Weiss DJ, Cameron E, Bisanzio D, Mappin B, Dalrymple U, et al. The effect of malaria control on Plasmodium falciparum in Africa between 2000 and 2015. Nature. 2015 Oct 8;526(7572):207–11.
14. Lengeler C. Insecticide-treated bed nets and curtains for preventing malaria. Cochrane Database Syst Rev. 2004;(2):CD000363.
15. Banteyerga H. Ethiopia's health extension program: improving health through community involvement. MEDICC Rev. 2011 Jul;13(3):46–9.
16. Workie N, Ramana G. Ethiopia – The health extension program in Ethiopia [Internet]. World Bank; 2013 [cited 2026 Feb 16]. Available from: https://documents.worldbank.org/en/publication/documents-reports/documentdetail/356621468032070256
17. Tekle MG, Wolde HM, Medhin G, Teklu AM, Alemayehu YK, Gebre EG, et al. Understanding the factors affecting attrition and intention to leave of health extension workers: a mixed methods study in Ethiopia. Hum Resour Health. 2022 Feb 19;20(1):20.
18. Wolde HM, Tekle MG, Alemayehu YK, Gebre EG, Teklu AM. Attrition of health extension workers in Ethiopia: trends, regional variations and determinants – a mixed methods study of 15 years of experience. BMC Health Serv Res. 2023 Dec 20;23(1):1444.
19. Lenzer J. Secret report surfaces showing that Pfizer was at fault in Nigerian drug tests. BMJ. 2006 May 27;332(7552):1233.
20. Brilliant LB. The management of smallpox eradication in India [Internet]. University of Michigan Press; 1985. Available from: https://www.zero-pox.info/other_docs/brilliant_mgmt_spox_india.pdf
21. Greenough P. Intimidation, coercion and resistance in the final stages of the South Asian Smallpox Eradication Campaign, 1973–1975. Soc Sci Med. 1995 Sep;41(5):633–45.

13 Leading Without Command

Governing Distributed Power

If judgment defines leadership at scale, institutional structure defines its limits. The environments in which large-scale health initiatives unfold are not governed by a single authority. Power is distributed across sovereign states, multilateral agencies, donors, private manufacturers, regulatory bodies, civil society organizations, and communities. Incentives diverge, accountability is fragmented, and no single actor commands the system in its entirety.

Health systems research has long emphasized that policy implementation occurs within political and institutional arenas shaped by competing interests and uneven power.[1] Scaling a health intervention, therefore, is not merely a technical exercise; it is an act of navigating distributed authority within what political theorists describe as polycentric governance systems.[2] In such systems, multiple centers of decision-making coexist, formally autonomous yet functionally interdependent. Collective action depends less on command than on negotiated alignment.

Leadership in these settings cannot rely on hierarchy alone. It must operate through influence rather than instruction, negotiation rather than decree, and legitimacy rather than enforcement. Technical expertise does not guarantee compliance. Financing does not ensure coordination. Political endorsement does not eliminate institutional friction. Scale advances only when actors, each constrained by their own mandates and incentives, move in sufficiently aligned directions to sustain collective effort.

Across eradication campaigns, vaccine partnerships, and community health reforms, a consistent structural pattern emerges. Global eradication campaigns required international organizations to influence sovereign states without possessing sovereignty.[3] Vaccine partnerships depended on reconciling public health objectives with commercial realities. Community health reforms succeeded not because a single leader controlled every lever, but because institutional arrangements redistributed responsibility while preserving coherence. Even during crisis response, coordination operated through fragile coalitions rather than centralized command.[4]

In such environments, leadership becomes a problem of design rather than direction. The central questions shift from "Who decides?" to "How are incentives structured?" and from "Who commands?" to "How is alignment stabilized across autonomous actors?" Durable scale depends not on concentration of authority, but on institutional arrangements that make cooperation rational and defection costly.

DOI: 10.4324/9781003685821-18

Power Is Distributed, Not Centralized

Large-scale health initiatives operate within polycentric systems in which authority is dispersed across overlapping jurisdictions and institutional domains.[2] The structure illustrated in Figure 13.1 makes visible a core constraint of scale: authority is distributed rather than centralized.

Large-scale health initiatives operate within networks of semi-autonomous actors whose authority is overlapping rather than hierarchical. Influence flows in multiple directions. No single institution commands the system in its entirety.

Ministries regulate but depend on financing. Donors finance but lack sovereign mandate. Multilateral agencies convene but cannot compel compliance. Private manufacturers control production but respond to market incentives. Communities ultimately determine adoption and legitimacy.

In such polycentric systems, influence substitutes for command. Coordination emerges from negotiated alignment among actors who retain autonomy.

Understanding this distribution of authority is a prerequisite for effective leadership. Before mobilizing action, leaders must map who holds formal authority, who controls resources, who shapes narratives, and who can obstruct implementation.

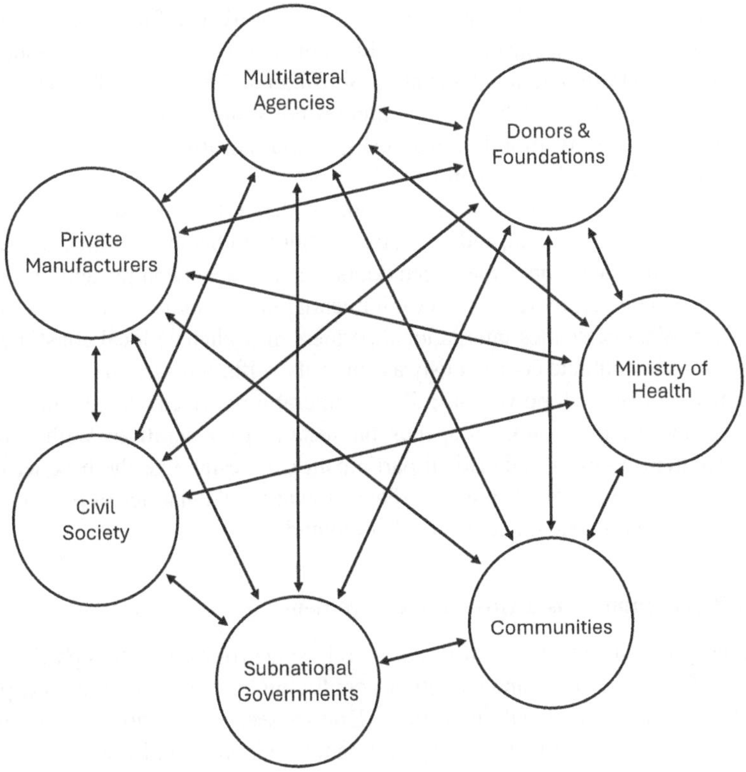

Figure 13.1 Distributed Authority in Polycentric Scale Systems

Scale succeeds not when power is consolidated, but when distributed authority is governed deliberately.

In such settings, formal mandate does not equal operational control. A global strategy does not guarantee local compliance. International organizations may convene actors, provide technical guidance, and mobilize resources, yet they cannot compel sovereign states to implement policy. As Barrett (2007) argues in his analysis of smallpox eradication, collective action problems persist even when actors share a common objective.[3] Eradication required sustained cooperation among states that retained ultimate autonomy.

The leadership of D.A. Henderson during the smallpox eradication campaign illustrates this constraint vividly. Although often portrayed as directing a global effort, Henderson possessed no sovereign authority over member states. The World Health Organization (WHO) could convene, recommend, and coordinate, but national governments retained ultimate decision-making power. Progress depended on persuading ministries to adopt surveillance-containment strategies, negotiating compliance across diverse political systems, and sustaining legitimacy in contexts where external oversight was sensitive.[5] The campaign's success derived not from centralized command, but from disciplined influence within a distributed system.

This dispersion of authority reshapes leadership fundamentally. Rather than issuing directives within a hierarchy, leaders must cultivate influence across institutional boundaries. They must negotiate alignment among actors whose cooperation is voluntary, conditional, and reversible. Shiffman and Smith (2007) demonstrate that political priority in global health emerges not simply from evidence but from the ability of actors to mobilize networks, shape narratives, and institutionalize commitments across dispersed arenas of power.[6]

First, influence substitutes for command. Leaders rely on persuasion, coalition-building, reputational capital, and normative authority rather than enforcement mechanisms. Technical legitimacy may open doors, but it does not compel action. Second, authority becomes contextual. An actor influential in one domain may be peripheral in another. What persuades international partners may alienate local constituencies. Leaders must recalibrate continuously as authority shifts across arenas.

Finally, distributed power amplifies vulnerability. Because no single actor controls the system, progress depends on sustained cooperation. Withdrawal or disengagement by even one critical participant can destabilize the broader effort. Leading at scale therefore requires vigilance toward the dynamics of power dispersion rather than reliance on centralized command.

Incentive Alignment as a Governance Problem

If authority is distributed, incentives are rarely synchronized. Actors participate in scaling efforts for distinct and sometimes conflicting reasons. Governments pursue political legitimacy and public welfare. Donors seek measurable returns within funding cycles. Private firms prioritize financial viability and risk management. Civil society organizations seek representation and equity. Communities value relevance, safety, and dignity.

Institutions shape behavior by structuring incentives.[7] Shared goals do not automatically produce aligned motivations. Scaling literature repeatedly demonstrates that technically sound interventions falter when incentives diverge.[8] The challenge is not merely to articulate common objectives but to engineer institutional arrangements that align behavior across actors with different mandates, particularly in contexts where financial and political incentives diverge across levels of the system.[9]

Temporal misalignment is a recurrent source of tension. Donor funding cycles may prioritize short-term results, while durable scale requires long-term maintenance. Political cycles may reward visible expansion but neglect system consolidation. Private manufacturers may respond to market volatility rather than long-term affordability commitments. As Pierson (2004) notes, political time horizons profoundly influence policy sustainability.[10] Leaders must therefore design mechanisms that bridge temporal gaps, ensuring continuity beyond electoral or funding cycles.

Risk allocation presents another challenge. When risk is unevenly distributed, cooperation erodes. If manufacturers bear disproportionate financial risk, supply becomes unstable. If governments absorb reputational risk without shared accountability, domestic support weakens. Governance arrangements must balance exposure sufficiently to sustain participation without inducing paralysis.[11] This requires deliberate design of contracts, procurement mechanisms, and regulatory frameworks.

The Meningitis Vaccine Project clearly illustrates these dynamics. Under the leadership of Marc LaForce, the partnership between WHO, PATH, African governments, and the Serum Institute of India required deliberate redistribution of financial and regulatory risk. Affordability targets, volume guarantees, and regulatory innovation were structured to make participation viable for a private manufacturer while preserving public health objectives. No single actor commanded the arrangement; instead, incentives were engineered so that cooperation became aligned with each participant's interest. The partnership's durability rested less on shared aspiration than on carefully aligned institutional design.

Accountability under fragmentation adds further complexity. When authority is dispersed, responsibility often diffuses. Failure invites blame-shifting rather than corrective action. Bovens (2007) emphasizes that accountability mechanisms are essential in complex governance arrangements to clarify who is answerable for which outcomes.[12] Without such clarity, coordination becomes fragile.

Incentive alignment, then, is not achieved through exhortation or shared rhetoric. It is institutionalized through carefully designed structures that reconcile divergent motivations. Leaders working at scale must act as architects of incentive systems, not merely advocates of common purpose.

From Personal Authority to Institutional Architecture

Max Weber's distinction between charismatic and rational-legal authority provides a useful lens.[13] Charismatic authority can inspire rapid mobilization but is inherently unstable. It depends on personal legitimacy and may dissipate with leadership transition. Rational-legal authority, embedded in institutional rules and procedures, provides continuity independent of individuals.

At scale, reliance on individual authority alone creates fragility. Political turnover, donor shifts, or executive transitions can unravel progress if institutional safeguards are absent. While individual leaders may catalyze reform, sustainable scale requires structures that endure beyond individual tenure.

Leadership at scale is often narrated through the lens of individual agency. Charismatic leaders, political champions, and visible institutional heads can catalyze change, mobilize attention, and signal urgency. These functions are indispensable, particularly in moments of crisis or reform. Yet the cases examined in this book show that while leader-centered authority can initiate scale, durable scale depends on institutional arrangements that stabilize incentives, distribute risk, and embed accountability beyond any single individual's tenure.

Table 13.1 contrasts a leader-centered authority model with an institutional design model across core governance dimensions relevant to multi-sector scale efforts.

Institutional design transforms momentum into durability by embedding authority, accountability, and continuity within governance arrangements. North (1990) argues that institutions reduce uncertainty by stabilizing expectations.[7] When roles, mandates, and accountability mechanisms are codified, coordination persists beyond individual tenure. The expansion of Ethiopia's Health Extension Program during ministerial reforms illustrates this principle. Rather than relying on charismatic mobilization, leadership embedded primary care expansion within formal workforce policy, standardized training, decentralized supervision, and salaried institutional roles. The durability of the program did not depend on a single reformer but on the codification of responsibilities across federal and regional structures. Scale was stabilized through institutionalization rather than personal authority.

Institutional design performs three stabilizing functions. First, it embeds continuity. Formal agreements, regulatory frameworks, and financing mechanisms endure across leadership transitions. Second, it distributes authority, preventing excessive dependence on any single actor. Third, it institutionalizes accountability, making performance evaluation routine rather than personality-driven.

This reframes the role of leaders. Their most consequential contributions may not be visible public acts but structural decisions that shape governance architecture.

Table 13.1 Leadership Models in Multi-Sector Scale Efforts

Dimension	*Leader-Centered Authority Model*	*Institutional Design Model*
Source of Stability	Personal credibility and charisma	Codified roles, rules, and agreements
Continuity	Dependent on individual tenure	Embedded in formal structures
Risk Management	Concentrated in leader	Distributed across institutions
Accountability	Informal, personality-driven	Formalized and procedural
Coalition Durability	Vulnerable to transition	Resilient to turnover
Sustainability of Scale	Accelerates early momentum	Stabilizes long-term impact

Designing procurement systems, establishing transparent oversight bodies, and codifying partnership agreements are acts of leadership that outlast charisma.

Scale driven primarily by individual momentum may accelerate quickly, but it requires institutional reinforcement to stabilize over time. By contrast, scale grounded in institutional design can withstand political and organizational turnover without systemic collapse. Leading without command therefore involves constructing structures that reduce dependence on personal authority.

Managing Multi-Sector Coalitions Under Constraint

Coalitions are the operational expression of distributed authority. Yet coalitions do not function simply because actors share goals. They function because coordination costs are actively managed and institutionalized.

Collaborative governance scholarship emphasizes that effective cross-sector coalitions require structured interaction, shared forums, and formalized decision rules.[14,15] In multi-sector health initiatives, actors confront informational asymmetry, resource imbalance, and political vulnerability.

Informational asymmetry arises because actors possess distinct forms of knowledge. Technical agencies hold epidemiological data. Governments control regulatory authority. Manufacturers control production information. Transparency must be balanced with proprietary or sovereign interests. Leaders must create shared visibility sufficient for coordination without undermining trust.

Resource imbalance introduces further tension. Donors may control financing but lack implementation authority. Governments may possess mandate but face fiscal constraints. Private firms may possess technical capacity yet confront reputational risk. Coalition stability depends on arrangements that prevent dominance while preserving efficiency.

Political vulnerability adds volatility. Electoral shifts, geopolitical tensions, or public controversy can destabilize coalitions. Formal agreements, rather than informal trust alone, provide resilience. Keohane and Nye's (1977) theory of interdependence highlights how cooperation persists when institutions reduce transaction costs and provide predictable expectations.[16]

Coalition leadership, therefore, involves continuous recalibration. Alignment is dynamic, not static. Agreements must be revisited as conditions change. Legitimacy must be reaffirmed across constituencies. Disagreement is inevitable; fragmentation is not. Leaders must tolerate contestation while protecting core alignment.

Managing multi-sector coalitions under constraint is not about achieving consensus. It is about sustaining sufficient coherence among actors with divergent interests so that collective action remains possible.

Leadership Moves

Leading without command requires disciplined influence within systems of distributed authority. The moves that follow show how leaders can map power, align incentives, distribute risk, and stabilize cooperation when no single actor can compel collective action.

- **Map power before setting strategy.** Formal mandate rarely equals operational control. Effective leaders identify where sovereignty resides, who controls financing, where legitimacy is anchored, and where participation is voluntary. Strategy follows influence, not title.
- **Design incentives, not just declarations of alignment.** Shared purpose does not ensure coordinated behavior. Durable cooperation requires structuring financial exposure, redistributing risk, and crafting agreements so participation is rational for each actor. Alignment must be engineered.
- **Institutionalize reform beyond individuals.** Charisma may mobilize momentum, but institutions sustain it. Leaders translate initiative into codified roles, formal agreements, and durable governance arrangements that outlast personal tenure.
- **Distribute risk deliberately.** When regulatory, financial, or reputational exposure is concentrated in one actor, cooperation erodes. Risk must be allocated across institutions in ways that preserve participation and protect legitimacy.
- **Stabilize coalitions through structure.** Trust enables collaboration, but formal mechanisms sustain it. Transparent accountability, written agreements, and predictable decision rules protect alignment under political and economic strain.

References

1. Gilson L. Health policy and systems research: a methodology reader: the abridged version [Internet]. Geneva: World Health Organization; 2012. Available from: https://iris.who.int/server/api/core/bitstreams/32fc3903-1361-4690-aaa3-c08ced2f1400/content
2. Ostrom E. Governing the commons: the evolution of institutions for collective action. Cambridge; New York: Cambridge University Press; 1990. 280 p. (The political economy of institutions and decisions).
3. Barrett S. The smallpox eradication game. Public Choice. 2007 Jan 1;130(1):179–207.
4. Moon S, Ruiz AA, Vieira M. Averting future vaccine injustice. New England Journal of Medicine. 2021 Jul 14;385(3):193–6.
5. Fenner F, Henderson DA, Arita I, Ježek Z, Ladnyi ID. Smallpox and its eradication [Internet]. Geneva, Switzerland: World Health Organization; 1988 [cited 2026 Feb 13]. Available from: https://iris.who.int/items/ba4ab312-1c43-4304-8235-969979499717
6. Shiffman J, Smith S. Generation of political priority for global health initiatives: a framework and case study of maternal mortality. The Lancet. 2007 Oct 13;370(9595):1370–9.
7. North DC. Institutions, institutional change, and economic performance. Cambridge; New York: Cambridge University Press; 1990. 152 p. (The political economy of institutions and decisions).
8. Yamey G. Scaling up global health interventions: a proposed framework for success. PLOS Medicine. 2011 Jun 28;8(6):e1001049.
9. Mangham LJ, Hanson K. Scaling up in international health: what are the key issues? Health Policy Plan. 2010 Mar 1;25(2):85–96.

10. Pierson P. Politics in time: history, institutions, and social analysis [Internet]. Princeton University; 2004 [cited 2026 Feb 13]. Available from: https://press.princeton.edu/books/paperback/9780691117157/politics-in-time
11. Williamson OE. The new institutional economics: taking stock, looking ahead. Journal of Economic Literature. 2000 Sep;38(3):595–613.
12. Bovens M. Analysing and assessing accountability: a conceptual framework. European Law Journal. 2007;13(4):447–68.
13. Weber M. Economy and society: an outline of interpretive sociology. Oakland, CA: University of California Press; 1978.
14. Ansell C, Gash A. Collaborative governance in theory and practice. J Public Adm Res Theory. 2008 Oct 1;18(4):543–71.
15. Emerson K, Nabatchi T, Balogh S. An integrative framework for collaborative governance. J Public Adm Res Theory. 2012 Jan 1;22(1):1–29.
16. Keohane RO, Nye JS. Power and interdependence. 4th ed. Boston: Longman; 1977. 330 p.

14 Designing the Leadership Ecosystem for Scale

The Reproduction Problem

If scale depends on disciplined judgment and structural governance, then leadership cannot be treated as an incidental byproduct of technical training. It must be reproduced intentionally. Yet global health rarely interrogates how leadership itself is generated, legitimized, and sustained across generations.

The question is not simply how to improve individual competence. It is how leadership capacity is reproduced through institutional design. Who is selected, credentialed, funded, made visible, and invited into agenda-setting spaces determines not only who leads, but what kinds of leadership become possible.

Institutions do more than coordinate action. They confer legitimacy. Fellowship programs, academic credentials, multilateral appointments, and donor-funded initiatives shape who is authorized to speak for global health and whose knowledge counts as expertise. Leadership pathways are not neutral pipelines. They are mechanisms of recognition and exclusion.

These pathways are structured by political economy. Funding flows influence which leadership programs are resourced. Institutional prestige shapes whose ideas circulate. Language dominance affects whose research travels. Over time, these dynamics narrow epistemic and geographic diversity even as formal training opportunities expand.

The paradox is subtle. As global health has professionalized, leadership pathways have become more structured. Structure can increase coordination and technical rigor. It can also consolidate authority within a limited set of institutions and regions. Systems designed to stabilize leadership may inadvertently reproduce hierarchy.

If Chapter 12 examined the discipline of judgment and Chapter 13 explored the governance of distributed power, a prior question emerges: Who becomes capable of exercising that discipline and navigating that structure? The answer lies not only in talent or motivation, but in how leadership ecosystems are designed.

Leadership at scale is not only practiced. It is reproduced. Figure 14.1 illustrates leadership as a nested ecosystem rather than an individual attribute. Governance capacity sits at the center, shaped by development pathways, gatekeeping structures, and the broader political economy that defines legitimacy and authority.

DOI: 10.4324/9781003685821-19

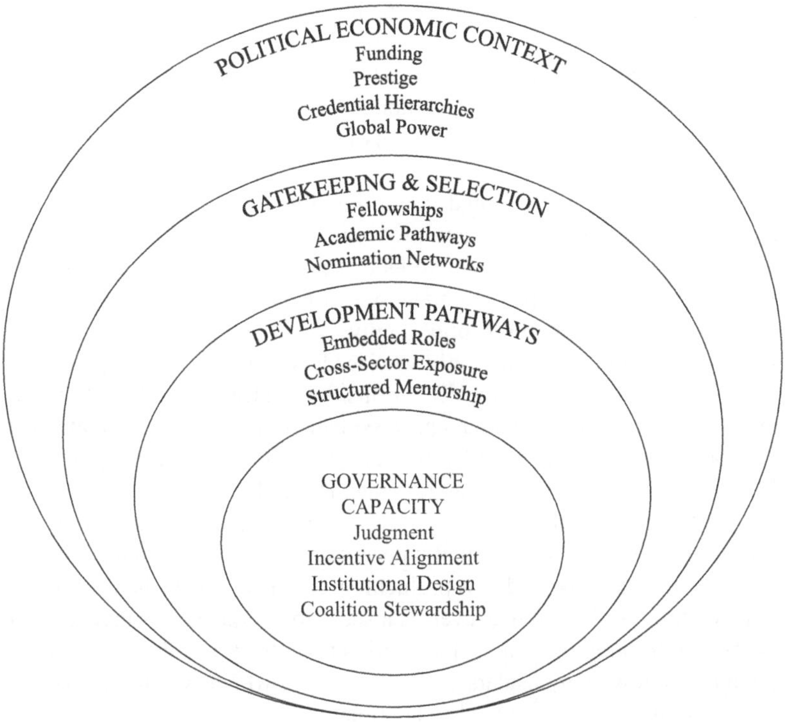

Figure 14.1 The Leadership Ecosystem for Scale

The unit of analysis shifts from leader qualities to pipeline design. Durable scale depends on that shift.

Leadership capacity at scale is nested within a broader ecosystem. Governance capacity is shaped by development pathways, gatekeeping structures, and political economy conditions that determine who is selected, authorized, and sustained in positions of authority.

The Architecture of Gatekeeping

Leadership reproduction operates through identifiable filters. Access to prestigious institutions, fellowship nominations, global conferences, multilateral appointments, and advisory boards is often mediated by existing networks of recognition. Selection criteria may appear meritocratic, yet merit is defined within institutional cultures that privilege particular credentials, languages, and career trajectories.[1,2]

These filters accumulate. Early access to well-resourced universities expands research funding opportunities. Funding increases publication visibility. Visibility expands eligibility for global panels and committees. Each stage appears procedural. Collectively, they structure the architecture of leadership. This pattern reflects cumulative advantage: early institutional capital amplifies subsequent opportunity.[3]

The result is not exclusion by design. It is reproduction by pattern. Leadership ecosystems elevate those already positioned within established circuits of authority. Emerging leaders outside these circuits face additional barriers to recognition, regardless of capability.

Early in my career, I assumed credibility followed competence. Over time, I learned that credibility also follows proximity: proximity to well-resourced institutions, global convenings, and networks that nominate rather than invite through open processes. The system is not malicious. It is patterned. Once visible, the pattern reshapes how one interprets opportunity.

This dynamic influences not only who leads, but how leadership is practiced. When pipelines are geographically or institutionally concentrated, leadership norms standardize around dominant professional cultures. Decision-making styles, risk tolerance, and definitions of legitimacy reflect embedded assumptions.

The deeper issue is epistemic range. When leadership pathways narrow, so does the range of lived experience shaping governance decisions. Research on political priority formation demonstrates that whose voices are institutionalized influences which issues gain traction and how problems are framed.[4] Scale then unfolds within constrained frames of reference, even as it seeks to operate across diverse contexts.

Expanding training programs alone will not resolve this imbalance. The central question is not how many leaders are produced, but which systems authorize them and whose authority is recognized as legitimate.

Why Traditional Leadership Development Is Insufficient for Scale

Most leadership development initiatives focus on individual growth. They strengthen communication, strategic planning, negotiation, and personal effectiveness. These competencies are essential. They form the foundation of leadership practice. Yet they do not fully address the structural architecture through which leadership is authorized and sustained at scale.

Traditional programs often assume that better-trained individuals will naturally produce better outcomes. In stable environments, that assumption may hold. But scale unfolds within systems where authority is fragmented, incentives diverge, and legitimacy is contested. Without preparing leaders to navigate these structural conditions, training can produce technically proficient actors who are not fully equipped for governance under constraint.

Four limitations tend to persist.

First, institutional literacy is underemphasized. Participants may learn how to persuade or manage teams, but not how to design governance arrangements, structure accountability, or redistribute risk across actors. Institutional scholarship reminds us that behavior is shaped less by intention than by the rules and incentives embedded within systems.[2,5] Scale requires literacy in those structures.

Second, distributed authority is under-taught. Programs often assume a clear chain of command. In practice, leadership at scale operates across sovereign governments, multilateral institutions, private firms, and civil society actors who retain autonomy. Polycentric governance research demonstrates that collective action depends on alignment across semi-autonomous actors rather than hierarchical control.[6] Few curricula train leaders to map power across such systems before acting within them.

Third, complexity exposure is too shallow. Emerging leaders are frequently shielded from ambiguity rather than trained to operate within it. Simulations emphasize clarity and decisiveness rather than disciplined uncertainty and provisional judgment. Adaptive leadership scholarship emphasizes that complex challenges cannot be solved through technical expertise alone and require mobilizing people to confront difficult trade-offs.[7]

Fourth, leadership is over-framed as transferable skill rather than contextual practice. What works within one institutional culture may not translate across sectors or regions. Systems theory underscores that outcomes emerge from interactions among interdependent actors rather than isolated decisions.[8] Without structured cross-sector and cross-geographic experience, leaders risk mistaking familiarity for universality.

These limitations do not invalidate existing leadership programs. They reveal a deeper gap. Leadership at scale is not only personal effectiveness. It is governance capacity within distributed systems.

If leadership ecosystems reproduce hierarchy and training models emphasize individual competence without structural fluency, then designing the next generation requires rebalancing both selection and preparation. The goal is not to produce more leaders. It is to cultivate leaders capable of exercising judgment under uncertainty and governing distributed power.

For scale-capable leadership to be reproduced, development must deliberately cultivate two intertwined capacities: disciplined judgment under uncertainty and governance across distributed authority.

The sections that follow outline what it takes to cultivate these capacities and how pipelines can be designed to position leaders where authority is actually exercised.

Developing Judgment Under Uncertainty

Chapter 12 argued that leadership at scale is defined less by certainty than by disciplined judgment under conditions of incomplete information, contested authority, and uneven consequences. The cases examined throughout this book demonstrated that leaders do not act because uncertainty disappears. They act because delay would compound risk. They decide without full clarity. They revise without surrendering direction. They accept moral residue—the ethical weight that remains after difficult decisions—without retreating into procedural neutrality.

The question for leadership development is therefore not whether uncertainty can be eliminated, but how judgment under uncertainty can be cultivated.

First, leaders must learn to decide with incomplete information. In complex health systems, data are partial, delayed, or politically filtered. Evidence evolves. Stakeholders disagree. Waiting for consensus may be infeasible. Training that rewards precision without ambiguity inadvertently prepares leaders for stable environments that rarely exist at scale. Development must therefore incorporate structured exposure to ambiguous decision environments where trade-offs are explicit and information is insufficient. Case-based deliberation, real-time policy simulation, and supervised responsibility for live institutional decisions create conditions in which provisional action becomes normalized rather than feared.

Second, leaders must learn to distinguish between reversible and irreversible decisions. Some policy choices can be corrected with limited systemic disruption. Others embed long-term structural consequences. Scale intensifies this distinction because institutional reforms, procurement arrangements, and governance design often persist beyond leadership tenure. Developing this discrimination requires reflective analysis of historical interventions, including those that needed mid-course correction and those whose rigidity generated fragility. Leaders must be trained not only to ask what decision to make, but which consequences they are prepared to own.

Third, leaders must learn to carry moral residue. Ethical leadership at scale is not the elimination of harm but the management of trade-offs. Allocation decisions privilege some populations over others. Regulatory innovation redistributes risk. Institutional reform benefits some actors while constraining others. Leadership development must therefore extend beyond compliance training toward ethical reflection grounded in accountability. Structured discussion of contested cases fosters the discipline of naming trade-offs explicitly rather than masking them behind procedure.

Fourth, leaders must learn to act provisionally. Strategy at scale is iterative. Plans are hypotheses subject to revision. Adaptive leadership scholarship emphasizes that complex challenges require experimentation and learning rather than linear execution.[7] Similarly, systems theory underscores that outcomes emerge from dynamic interaction rather than static design.[8] Development programs that reward unwavering confidence over adaptive recalibration risk producing rigidity rather than resilience.

Cultivating judgment under uncertainty requires shifting evaluation metrics within leadership development itself. Rather than assessing participants solely on decisiveness or rhetorical clarity, programs must value structured reasoning, acknowledgment of trade-offs, and willingness to revise. Emerging leaders should be encouraged to articulate assumptions, surface blind spots, and anticipate unintended consequences.

Judgment is not innate. It is developed through exposure to constraint, accountability for decisions, and guided reflection on outcomes. Leadership ecosystems that insulate emerging leaders from complexity delay this development. Ecosystems that embed leaders within real institutional tensions accelerate it.

If scale demands disciplined reasoning under uncertainty, then leadership development must be designed around uncertainty rather than protected from it.

Training for Distributed Power

If judgment under uncertainty defines how leaders think, distributed authority defines where they must act. Chapter 13 demonstrated that scale unfolds within polycentric systems in which no actor commands the whole. Ministries regulate but depend on financing. Donors finance but lack sovereign mandate. Multilateral agencies convene but cannot compel compliance. Private manufacturers respond to market incentives rather than public health objectives. Communities determine legitimacy and adoption. Leadership in such systems is not the exercise of authority. It is the governance of distributed power.

Leadership development must therefore prepare emerging leaders to operate within these structural realities.

First, leaders must learn to map power before mobilizing action. In the smallpox eradication campaign, global coordination depended not on formal authority but on persuading sovereign governments to adopt surveillance-containment strategies. The central office could convene and recommend, but compliance remained voluntary. Leadership development that assumes hierarchical command would fail to prepare leaders for such terrain. Power mapping must become a core competency. Emerging leaders should be trained to identify where authority resides, who controls resources, whose consent is necessary, and where resistance is likely to emerge.

Second, leaders must learn to align incentives rather than rely on shared rhetoric. The Meningitis Vaccine Project succeeded not simply because actors agreed on the importance of meningitis control, but because financial, regulatory, and production incentives were structured deliberately to make participation rational for each partner. Affordability targets, volume guarantees, and regulatory innovation redistributed risk across institutions so that cooperation was sustainable. Leadership programs that focus solely on communication skills without teaching incentive design leave leaders unprepared for such governance challenges. Training must include exposure to contract structuring, procurement mechanisms, regulatory negotiation, and financial risk allocation.

Third, leaders must learn to design institutions that stabilize coordination beyond personal authority. During the COVID-19 vaccine rollout, coordination required temporary platforms, regulatory adaptations, and hybrid governance arrangements that extended across national and international actors. In many settings, success depended less on charismatic leadership than on the rapid construction of decision forums, oversight mechanisms, and accountability structures capable of operating under pressure. Leadership development must therefore cultivate institutional design literacy. Participants should learn how to structure memoranda of understanding, clarify accountability lines, and embed decision processes that endure beyond crisis moments.

Fourth, leaders must learn to manage coalitions under constraint. Distributed systems generate informational asymmetry, resource imbalance, and political vulnerability. In each of the cases examined in this book, progress required sustaining cooperation among actors with divergent mandates. Coalition management is not consensus-building alone. It is the disciplined maintenance of alignment when incentives diverge and pressures intensify. Collaborative governance scholarship underscores the importance of structured interaction and formalized decision rules in sustaining such partnerships.[9] Leadership curricula must therefore move beyond interpersonal communication to include governance architecture and coalition stabilization.

Most leadership programs teach persuasion. Few teach institutional engineering. Yet scale depends on the latter.

Training for distributed power requires immersing emerging leaders in cross-sector environments. Rotations across government, multilateral organizations, private sector entities, and civil society platforms cultivate the ability to interpret incentives across domains. Embedded placements within regulatory agencies or financing bodies expose leaders to the structural levers that shape behavior. Simulated negotiations that incorporate competing mandates and asymmetric risk sharpen structural fluency.

If smallpox revealed the limits of centralized authority, if MenAfriVac demonstrated the power of incentive alignment, and if COVID-19 exposed the fragility and necessity of coalition governance under pressure, then leadership development must internalize these lessons. Preparing leaders for distributed systems means teaching them not only how to influence people, but how to design structures that make alignment durable.

Leadership at scale is not a performance. It is a governance practice. Training must reflect that reality.

Building Institutional Pipelines, Not Just Individuals

Several years ago, a young public health officer was selected for a prestigious global fellowship and embedded within a headquarters-based technical advisory working group. She had strong academic credentials, impressive field experience, and a clear commitment to health equity. During the fellowship year, she attended high-level meetings, contributed to procurement reform discussions, produced policy briefs, and expanded her professional network. By every formal metric, the program was a success.

Two years later, she returned to a ministry role in her home country. The networks she had built were difficult to activate from outside global headquarters. She did not control budgets, hold signature authority, or set agenda priorities. The policy frameworks she had learned did not translate easily into local political realities. Domestic fiscal constraints and donor reporting cycles shaped what was feasible. The fellowship had expanded her visibility and confidence, but it had not altered the formal distribution of authority within which she operated.

This was not a failure of talent. It was a failure of pipeline design. The pattern repeats: talent expands, authority does not.

If leadership is reproduced structurally, then development cannot rely on isolated programs or charismatic mentorship alone. Sustainable scale requires institutional pipelines that cultivate, position, and retain leaders across diverse health systems.

Traditional leadership development often centers on discrete experiences: a fellowship year, a short executive course, a global workshop. They rarely alter the structural pathways through which authority is conferred and sustained. Without integration into institutional roles, decision-making platforms, and governance structures, leadership development remains episodic.

Institutional pipelines, by contrast, embed leadership cultivation within organizational ecosystems. They connect training to trajectory.

Leadership fellowships can serve as entry points into such pipelines, but only when they link participants to real decision environments and long-term institutional roles. Classroom instruction must be paired with embedded placements in ministries, regional public health bodies, financing institutions, or multilateral agencies where governance is negotiated under constraint. Exposure to live institutional tension accelerates structural literacy. Emerging leaders learn not only how policy is written, but how it is funded, contested, and revised.

Cross-sector rotations deepen this learning. Leaders who move between government, academia, private industry, and civil society begin to see how incentives shift across domains. They learn that a procurement decision is also a political decision, that regulatory reform reshapes market behavior, and that community legitimacy can override formal authority. Such mobility builds coalition fluency and strengthens alignment capacity in polycentric systems, where coordination depends on interaction among semi-autonomous actors rather than centralized control.[6]

Intergenerational mentorship remains essential, but it must extend beyond informal advice. Senior leaders transmit tacit knowledge about navigating distributed authority, absorbing reputational risk, and sustaining legitimacy when guidance must change publicly. When mentorship is structured within institutional pathways rather than left to informal proximity, leadership reproduction becomes less dependent on access to elite networks.

Pipeline breadth is equally critical. Leadership ecosystems that draw disproportionately from a narrow set of institutions or regions risk narrowing the range of judgment and experience available for decision-making. When agenda-setting bodies are composed primarily of leaders socialized within similar professional cultures, policy framing becomes standardized even across diverse contexts. Research on political priority formation demonstrates that whose voices are institutionalized influences which problems gain traction and how they are framed.[4] Designing pipelines that cultivate talent across varied health systems strengthens legitimacy and enhances adaptive capacity.

Institutional pipelines also stabilize continuity. Leadership transitions are inevitable. Without structured succession pathways, reforms become vulnerable to turnover. With intentional pipelines, succession becomes deliberate. Leaders step into roles already familiar with governance architecture, coalition dynamics, and system constraints. Institutional memory is preserved. Reform momentum does not depend on a single personality. Institutional scholarship emphasizes that continuity depends on the codification of roles and expectations rather than individual tenure alone.[2,10]

The goal is not to manufacture uniform leaders. It is to design ecosystems in which diverse leaders are prepared systematically for roles that require judgment under uncertainty and governance across distributed power.

Scale endures when leadership reproduction is intentional. It falters when leadership emergence is accidental.

The Leadership Ecosystem for Global Health

Designing leadership ecosystems for scale requires redefining legitimate authority. In distributed governance systems, legitimacy is operational. When decision-making bodies reflect a narrow range of geographic, professional, or institutional backgrounds, policy may remain technically coherent while becoming socially brittle. Scale depends as much on perceived legitimacy and credible participation as on technical coordination.

Composition shapes governance outcomes. Who sits in agenda-setting forums influences which problems are prioritized, which solutions are considered feasible, and whose risks are deemed acceptable. When pipelines privilege a limited set of credentials, languages, or institutional affiliations, epistemic range narrows. The field may become more standardized, but it becomes less adaptive.

Redesigning leadership pathways is therefore structural work. It requires altering who gains access to agenda-setting spaces, how credibility is conferred, and where resources are concentrated. Regional institutions must function as decision centers rather than feeder systems. Rotational appointments should embed emerging leaders within sovereign and regional governance bodies. Operational and community-based expertise must be recognized alongside academic credentials. Selection processes must move beyond closed nomination networks toward transparent and distributed access. The goal is not symbolic inclusion. It is distributed authority that reflects the system leaders are expected to govern.

Leadership ecosystems must mirror the conditions of scale. If authority is distributed, pipelines must be distributed. If legitimacy is contested, participation must be built into governance. If uncertainty is permanent, exposure to complexity must be structured intentionally.

Leadership Moves

Designing leadership ecosystems for scale requires more than expanding opportunities. It requires institutional architecture that reproduces governance capacity across people, places, and generations.

- **Reproduce governance capacity, not charisma.** Prioritize institutional literacy, accountability design, and decision architecture over personal prominence. Durable scale depends on leaders who understand systems, not simply those who command attention. Reward leaders who can redesign roles, incentives, and decision processes so reform survives beyond individual tenure.

- **Train judgment in real ambiguity.** Evaluate structured reasoning, trade-off management, and adaptive revision rather than confidence alone. Scale rewards disciplined uncertainty. Assessment criteria should value the articulation of assumptions, acknowledgment of risk, and willingness to revise under scrutiny.
- **Teach power as structure.** Make power mapping, incentive alignment, and coalition governance core curriculum. Influence at scale is engineered through institutional design. Leaders must learn to identify where authority resides, how compliance is negotiated, and how risk is distributed across actors.
- **Build pipelines, not episodes.** Link fellowships and executive programs to institutional roles, succession pathways, and durable placements. Leadership reproduction must be integrated into career trajectories, not delivered as a discrete experience. Development should alter formal authority pathways, not simply expand professional exposure.
- **Broaden recognized authority.** Redesign selection networks, credential norms, and agenda-setting authority so leadership reflects the systems it must govern. Legitimacy strengthens when decision-making bodies include the institutional, operational, and contextual knowledge needed for scale.

Leadership ecosystems determine who is prepared to exercise judgment and who is authorized to govern distributed power. Narrow ecosystems produce brittle scale. Distributed ecosystems produce durable scale.

Across this book, scale has not meant expansion alone. It has meant constraint: fragmented authority, persistent uncertainty, intensifying trade-offs, and systems under strain. What endures is not technical brilliance but disciplined governance.

If leadership at scale is judgment under uncertainty and coordination without command, then the decisive question is structural: Who is prepared to exercise that judgment, and through what pathways are they authorized to do so?

Leadership ecosystems answer that question long before crisis arrives. They determine whose expertise is recognized, whose perspectives shape agendas, whose institutions receive investment, and how authority is treated as legitimate.

The future of global health will not be determined by technological innovation. It will be determined by whether leadership pathways reproduce governance capacity across generations, regions, and institutions. Leaders capable of allocating uncertainty, managing complexity, and remaining answerable for uneven consequences will not emerge accidentally. They will emerge when the systems that form them are built for scale.

References

1. Bourdieu P. The forms of capital. Westport, CT: Greenwood; 1986. 241–58 p.
2. North DC. Institutions, institutional change, and economic performance. Cambridge; New York: Cambridge University Press; 1990. 152 p. (The political economy of institutions and decisions).
3. Merton RK. The Matthew Effect in science. Science. 1968 Jan 5;159(3810):56–63.

4. Shiffman J, Smith S. Generation of political priority for global health initiatives: a framework and case study of maternal mortality. The Lancet. 2007 Oct 13;370(9595): 1370–9.
5. Williamson OE. The new institutional economics: taking stock, looking ahead. Journal of Economic Literature. 2000 Sep;38(3):595–613.
6. Ostrom E. Governing the commons: the evolution of institutions for collective action. Cambridge; New York: Cambridge University Press; 1990. 280 p. (The political economy of institutions and decisions).
7. Heifetz RA. Leadership without easy answers. Cambridge, MA: Belknap Press of Harvard University Press; 1994. 348 p.
8. Senge PM. The fifth discipline: the art and practice of the learning organization (Rev. ed.). New York: Doubleday; 2006.
9. Ansell C, Gash A. Collaborative governance in theory and practice. J Public Adm Res Theory. 2008 Oct 1;18(4):543–71.
10. Pierson P. Politics in time: history, institutions, and social analysis [Internet]. Princeton University; 2004 [cited 2026 Feb 13]. Available from: https://press.princeton.edu/books/paperback/9780691117157/politics-in-time

Index

Note: **Bold** page numbers refer to tables; *italic* page numbers refer to figures.